ANGELS CRYING

A True Story
of Secrecy and Tragedy

by

TOM MOORE

ISBN # 0-9698962-0-4

Printed and bound in Canada by Dicks and Company

cover by Gerald Squires
model Brenda Green
photo by Manfred Buchheit

Other books by Tom Moore:

Good-Bye Momma (Breakwater) a short novel
Sir Wilfred Grenfell (Fitzhenry & Whiteside) a children's biography
The Black Heart (Harry Cuff) poetry
Tomcods Kids & Confederation (Jesperson) a children's story

Copies may be ordered from:

Tomcod Press
8 Renews Street
St. John's, NF
Canada
A1E 3R8
709-368-4678

TOMCOD
PRESS

to my son, Tommy

CONTENTS

Preface

Tammy was a quiet, attractive girl who sat in my classroom in 1988. When I returned to school after that summer, they were taking her body out of the Atlantic Ocean. No one could tell me what had happened or why? There were rumours of suicide, murder, sexual assault, but there were no real answers, just that she was gone.

Tammy was a foster child, and no one seemed to be pursuing the obvious questions about her death. The silence was deafening.

Then a number of things happened that made this book possible. First the government set up a Royal Commission to look into sexual assaults at a local boys' home. Then the newly elected Liberal government expanded the purview of the Hughes Royal Commission to include foster homes. This gave public access to all files relating to children like Tammy whose case then came under the mandate of the commission. Her case files included documents of the RCMP, the Departments of Social Services, Justice and other agencies.

Thus began the project of my life: to research, write and publish this book. It is not just another book about sexual abuse. It is not about blame but about understanding what happened and the major role that secrecy and polite silence played in it. I have changed the names and disguised the locations of anyone who could be embarrassed by the truth. The dialogues are quoted from Royal Commission files, court transcripts, or faithfully approximated from personal interviews.

Tom Moore
St. John's, Newfoundland
October 2, 1994

Preface to 2nd edition

My Toronto agent offered poor comfort as I embarked on this project. She said, "If you try to publish a book by yourself you will have a full basement and an empty bank account." Cautious lawyers warned me of litigation and timid publishers referred me to more cautious lawyers.

But I could not see this book sitting on my shelf in manuscript form for another four years. The story had to be told and the ogre of secrecy challenged.

Support came from many different fronts: friends phoned to buy books and offered to sell copies for me; strangers phoned me in tears relating personal experiences; the Newfoundland and Labrador Arts Council funded a cross-island tour of the book; the Chair of Child Protection at MUN wrote a glowing review (see back cover); the Writers Alliance invited me to be their guest reader; the book sold out in five weeks.

Most media in Newfoundland saw the importance of increasing public understanding of such a complex topic. They wrote articles and did interviews about the book.

Like the polar ice cap, the horrible secrecy is slowly melting. Powerful walls of resistance endure, but I choose to believe that we are closer to the day when adults will be able to discuss sexual matters with the same ease that we discuss patio furniture and pot geraniums.

On that day our children will feel free to tell us in clear sexual words when someone does something bad to them. No longer will they be silenced and alone, as were the girls in my book, at the edge of the unknown sea of sexual language.

Tom Moore
St. John's, Newfoundland
December 5, 1994

Acknowledgements

Thanks to Tammy's family of origin who were most supportive and helpful, providing letters, photos, and encouragement.

People closest to me, especially Tommy, had to put up with me and my research for the last four years. Thank you for your patience and for taking my word that this book was worth it. Thanks to my school board for a term of unpaid leave and a year deferred salary leave.

Special thanks to Dawn Williams and Ann Wicks; Madeleine Morton; Joan Sullivan; Jane Urquhart; Ron Joy; David Hickey; Mike Coady; Betty Woodford; Gerald and Gail Squires; John Dalton; Gordon Rogers; Maggie Siggins; Vicky Rideout; Clay Powell; John Woodford; Herb Vivien; Joan Veitch; Linda Babstock; Tina Butt of Desktop Design; Brian Aylward; John Staple; Ron Pumphrey; Inspector Randy Hogg RCMP; Constable Randy Gallant RCMP; Superintendent Emerson Kaiser RCMP; Frank Gronach, Senior Crown Prosecutor, Newfoundland; Colin Flynn, Director of Public Prosecutions for Newfoundland; Brian Corbett; Honourable Madam Justice Marie Corbett; Sandy Simms, Supreme Court, Brigus; The Royal Commission of Inquiry into the Response of the Newfoundland Criminal Justice System to Complaints; Staff of the A.C. Hunter Library; Newfoundland Provincial Parks and Recreation; St. John's Weather Office; Grace Hospital Medical Records; St. Clare's Hospital Medical Records.

In spite of much assistance from these people any errors or omissions are entirely the fault of the author.

*CAST OF CHARACTERS

Tammy King - the main subject of this book
Maggie King - her younger sister
Allan Weller - the patriarch of the Weller family
Albert Weller - Tammy's foster father
Alice Weller - Tammy's foster mother
Levi Weller - Dawn William's foster father
Billy Weller - Levi Weller's son
Frank Weller - brother of Albert, Levi and Pat
Pat Weller - another brother
Ann Wicks - an earlier foster child of Albert Weller
Dawn Williams - an earlier foster child of Levi Weller
Edith Decker - Tammy's child welfare worker
Madonna Hynes - another child welfare worker
Constable Ron Green - the RCMP investigating officer

*Names have been changed.

CHAPTER 1

THE LAST DAY OF SUMMER

... Everything turns away
Quite leisurely from the disaster;
The plowman may have heard the splash,
The forsaken cry,
But for him it was not an important failure;
The sun shone
As it had to on the white legs
Disappearing into the green water ...

W.H. Auden, <u>Musée des Beaux Arts</u>

It was not a day for dying at Deep Harbour. True, the summer sun was losing its strength, but the soft wind from the west carried warmth from the land and brought it to the sea. The water in the harbour gleamed where the sun struck it and glowed the colour of the deepest, brightest blue; bluer than a child's eyes. It was very calm.

Down the harbour road, in a garage near the local church, two fishermen were building a box for the graveyard. They were brothers, both in their forties; pleasant men with quiet manners and strong hands that nailed the boards together.

Three feet deep, four feet long by two feet across, it was a wooden box, much like a small coffin, to be sunk in the graveyard, filled with cement and used to anchor the mast of a large cross. As well as fishermen, both were iron workers who had worked on the tall steel buildings of New York and Toronto, they were quite capable of the carpenter's task at hand.

Bob Dobbin was the older of the two brothers, a large, strong and heavy set man. John was taller and thinner, a youngish looking forty. They worked well together, relaxed and quiet.

Around 5 p.m. John went home for supper. The soft westerly wind that had been blowing across the harbour all day had stilled. The evening temperature had already begun to drop from a high of 17 towards the evening low of 9 degrees Celsius. The late afternoon sun shone between an occasional fluffy cumulus cloud.

John drove his truck along the road high over the westerly side of the harbour for the short distance to his own house. The blue waters of the harbour lay, as he later said, "clock calm" in the evening sun. As he neared home he waved to his daughter, Donna, riding her bike after her first day back at school. Summer was ending on a soft, long note.

As he turned into his yard he looked further up the harbour road past the church. The children of the harbour were around the community wharf. Some were on bikes. Others were jigging tomcods or an occasional flatfish; complaining when they snagged an unwelcome sculpin. Summer seemed to be offering another grand day before the school work and cool weather of fall were upon them.

But something much more ominous than cooler weather was about to settle on this quiet community. Even as the children played on the wharf, a drama between two people was being played out on the other side of the harbour. There, a secluded and almost inaccessible wooded lot faced the water directly over a 14 meter cliff. Near the edge of this cliff, a man and a fifteen year old girl were about to reach the climax of a strange relationship.

About 6 p.m. John returned to Bob's garage to resume work on the graveyard "form". The sky had clouded over and the evening air was cooling very quickly. While they were working, John thought he heard someone shouting. Neither he nor Bob mentioned it immediately. Then they heard a helicopter. It seemed to be flying low over the harbour, so the two men went out into Bob's yard. The RCMP helicopter was flying out over Rocky Cove Point, directly across the harbour.

"Probably someone after shooting a moose," Bob suggested as they returned to the work at hand.

Hardly had a hammer struck the next nail when they heard the muffled cries, "Help! Help!"

It was a man's voice. Back in the yard the two men looked in the direction of the harbour but could see nothing unusual. The helicopter was gone but they heard the faint cries for help again. "I'm going in the house for the binoculars," said Bob. Soon he was back and scanning the harbour for a capsized boat, or a fisherman in some peril.

The "way of the sea" in Newfoundland is a dangerous way, as novelist Norman Duncan so aptly recorded in 1903. The survival of fishermen for over three centuries at Deep Harbour depended on men like Bob and John looking out for each other when trouble occurred.

On the far shore of the harbour, off Rocky Cove Point his search stopped.

"There's a man in the water." He handed the binoculars to his brother. John looked and saw the first palpable evidence of the tragedy about to unfold.

At the water's edge, a man stood at the base of a cliff, up to his ankles in the sea water. "He must be trapped there by the tide."

"Is anyone on the way over to get him?" asked Bob.

"No, there's no one on the wharf now." The supper call had lured most of the locals to their homes.

"Let's go over and get him out of it," said Bob. "We'll take my boat; she's tied up at the wharf."

The two men drove quickly to the community wharf in John's truck. The wharf was deserted. A number of unconcerned, younger kids were playing in front of the fish plant. The men quickly untied Bob's boat and set off across the quiet water, a distance of about a kilometre. It was now around 7 p.m. The water was flat calm although the sky was cloudy.

Bob was in the stern manning the outboard motor while John perched in the bow peering ahead across a kilometre of open water. Soon he could clearly see the figure of a man at the edge of the shore on the other side of the harbour. The man was leaning backwards with one hand against the cliff face.

Bob warned, "Hold on now John, we don't know how dangerous this fellow might be. He could be in trouble or he could be right out of the "Mental". John reached for an oar.

"It's Albert Weller," John said, recognizing the man about his own age from the community. With adrenalin pumping, John sought a safe spot to land the boat. He was not ready for what he saw next. "Bob, boy, he's holding a body!"

The extended right arm of the stranded man held a female body by the wrist. The calm voice and the calm water belied the emotions racing through the two fishermen. John felt shock, disbelief and a cold, clammy dread.

Bob cut the engine. The water was so still that they floated quietly to just twenty feet from the stricken couple on the shore. There was an unreality about the scene.

Albert Weller was holding on to the girl in his right hand and with his left he leaned back against the cliff face. Searching up and down the shore, John could see it was the only place in sight where one could easily reach the water from the top. So sheer was the cliff that retreat had been impossible for the man, encumbered with the body. He was standing on a small ledge of cliff just under the water. She was floating, held by her arm. Her face half-submerged except when the swell of the tide ebbed.

Albert was wet and shivering from the cold. John also noticed that his face was purple.

"Give me her arm, now, Albert." John reached over the side and pulled the girl into the boat. Soon she lay supine in the bottom with her legs over the starboard gunwale.

Albert climbed in and John looked at the man crouched in the bow of the boat. "How did you get down there Albert? What happened?"

There was no reply.

"What happened?"

Albert just pointed to the cliff.

"Who is the girl?" John asked.

There was no reply.

"Who is she?" John demanded.

The reply was muffled. John could hear the one word: "King."

So it came to pass that the grim party of four made their way across Deep Harbour to the public wharf. It had become a dark, cool evening as the silent figures motored across the five minute expanse of water. The wet man, Albert, shivered in the front of the boat, then there was the dead girl on the bottom, next John looking at them, and lastly, Bob, at the motor in the stern. Each man was thinking his secret thoughts; each isolated by the drone of Bob's outboard engine.

People had already begun to gather on the wharf when the men arrived. A police officer met them from the four-man Baywood detachment of the Royal Canadian Mounted Police. He saw the body but instead addressed himself to Albert.

"Are you Albert Weller?"

A nod and a mumble acknowledged the fact.

"Come with me."

Then the officer said to the two fishermen, "This is the man we're after."

Then he helped Albert up out of the boat and led him by the arm to a police vehicle parked on the apron of the wharf.

John and Bob were left with the dead girl. A crowd had now gathered and the curious among them were peering down into the open boat to see the girl's body. Some of them recognized her and shock ran through the crowd.

Since it was summer, neither John nor Bob had a coat or blanket to cover the body so she remained exposed in the bottom of the boat.

John looked at his brother, "This is not right, her lying there like that."

Bob could only nod in agreement. "Yes. There's kids starting to come around too."

"Let's go get that cop," said John. He jumped up on the wharf and into the crowd of people who made way for the two large men. On the apron leading to the wharf they saw the RCMP van. As he walked toward it, John saw a frantic excitement reflected in the faces around him. The flashing red,

17

white and blue beacon lights directed their path through the growing crowd to the blue RCMP vehicle. The two brothers went around to the driver's side and John spoke through the open window to the officer. "You better get something to cover up the body."

Looking up, the officer said, "OK."

"The kids are starting to come around and we got nothing to cover her."

"OK," was the repeated reply.

They found a yellow tarpaulin and with that they covered the dead body still in the bottom of the boat with her feet over the gunwale.

John and Bob Dobbin waited by their boat with the curious crowd as evening gathered around the stricken wharf. Night was settling on Deep Harbour like a dark silk veil. It was becoming cold.

The two fishermen knew no answers to the murmured questions being quietly asked. Soon John stopped hearing them. He could see his neighbours turn their questioning faces to him. He watched their mouths open and close in what seemed like slow motion. Then he saw their faces turn back to the boat and its troubling cargo, only partly hidden by the yellow tarpaulin.

He gazed back across the harbour in the direction they had just come. The cliffs of Rocky Cove Point were almost invisible now, lost in the cool night mists.

A new chill was in the air. He rubbed his bare arms and knew that summer was finally and irrevocably over. No warmth came from the glare of the flashing lights atop the police van as they cut circles into the darkness of the still night.

The RCMP Investigation Report records the incidents of that evening:

> At 2005 hrs. a call was received at the RCMP office in Baywood from ***** ***** of Deep Harbour. He advised that he had seen a helicopter in the area and after it left he could hear calls for help coming from across the harbour. An immediate patrol was made to the *** residence by Constable Green.

It was learned that a local boat had just gone over to see what the trouble was. The boat could be seen at this time headed back towards the wharf in Deep Harbour with several people aboard. It was met as it pulled into the wharf. There were three males, one soaking wet, and the lifeless body of a female laying in the bottom of the boat. The male was observed sitting in the bow of the boat. He was dressed in shirt and pants and wearing work boots. He appeared to be very cold as he was crouched over and shaking.

The body of the female was observed laying face up with her head in the bilge area of the boat and her feet up and over the port gunwale. She was ashen in colour and was wearing a shirt and pants with white runners on her feet. Her clothing appeared to be intact on her body with no visible rips or buttons\zippers undone. She had no visible wounds.

The wet male was escorted to the police vehicle and determined through investigation to be Albert Weller. He advised that the girl was Tammy King. A call for assistance was made to guard the body and for crowd control. Assistance was obtained and Albert Weller was then removed from the scene to Baywood Detachment. He was obviously suffering from exposure so a doctor was requested. Sgt. Hilton attended the scene. Weller was advised that he was under arrest for involvement in the death of Tammy King at the RCMP office at 2057 hrs. He was lodged in cells and his clothing seized. Weller was cautioned and read his rights. He was asked what happened and all he would say is that the girl jumped off the cliff and that he jumped in after her in an attempt to save her.

19

The identity of the officer on the wharf is unclear. In fact, Albert was not arrested for involvement in Tammy's death as the RCMP report states. He was arrested for sexual assault against another girl, Ann Wicks. He was never charged with any wrongdoing against Tammy.

The report was signed by Constable Ronald Green, as events would later prove, a figure central to the tragedy.

Not far from the wharf that same evening Dr. John Waldo was at his clinic in Deep Harbour.

At nine o'clock Waldo received a phone call from the dispatcher at the RCMP detachment in Baywood. The female voice requested him to assist the officers at the public wharf in Deep Harbour. His exuberant personality can be read in the style of his report as he described the scene that followed:

> Within seconds I was on my way and found the area described, surrounded by multitudinous crowds, and following the glare in the dark of the RCMP rotating beacons, found myself at the well-patrolled wharf, where I was directed to the southern edge of the wharf extension. There were several RCMP officers who directed me to the wharf's edge and directed my attention to an open fishing boat lying hove to at the base of the wharf extension.

> The vessel was tied on to the wharf at what appeared to be relatively low tide. From the wharf, illuminated by multiple portable flashlights, the body of a person, identified to me by the attendant officers, lay in the scuppers of the boat, which already contained some 15 cm. of natural seawater, was identified to me as a person by the name of Tammy King, who had been dragged out of the cold water on the South side of Deep Harbour at some time between 2000 and 2028

hours immediately previously and had been ferried across the narrow inlet to the wharf. Unidentified onlookers claimed that there had been no movement of this person in an active motion in the previous hour.

Cursory examination from the wharfside showed a dark-haired, light complexioned prepubertal female of some 14 to 15 years lying cross-wise in the scuppers with face-up, head facing upwards, lying akimbo with the left ankle pointed up and over the starboard gunwale. This frail teenager showed no sign of natural movement, but was partially covered with a dry yellow cover and had already been presumed dead for the previous hour or so.

I descended into the boat to continue my investigation to find that indeed all life had passed from her. She was totally unresponsive to stimuli, her pupils were fully dilated, fixed and unresponsive to light. About 800 ml. of undisturbed finely divided froth was in front of her mouth and suggested death by drowning; her skin was cold to the touch, the muscles of her limbs were flaccid with the earliest hint of oncoming rigor mortis in the voluntary muscles; post mortem lividity gravitating to the dependant shoulders was already visible. Streaks of blood were evident on the medial side of her left arm and forearm but no obvious cause of local bleeding except for a small laceration on anterior left scalp which could have been either post- or pre-mortem in light of the interaction of the saltwater, any premortem landslide, or attempts to rescue the victim.

Close inspection of the neck and trunk revealed no immediate evidence of weapon use, nor of strangulation. The victim was soaking wet from head to foot but there was no evidence of premortem tampering with her clothing which was otherwise intact. Her top shirt showed no sign of violence, her brassiere was apparently undisturbed. She was wearing full-length trousers and there was no evidence of stress marks at the waist line. The top button of her slacks was in place, buttoned up, and showed no sign of foul play. Mark-abrasions on lateral forearm failed to contribute on cursory examination to violent intent.

She appeared to be dead for about an hour on the basis of the information available at the scene. Attempts at resuscitation were obviously beyond question at this time. I advised the senior RCMP at the site that a forensic autopsy should be performed to exclude other possible causes of death than simple drowning. I pronounced her deceased at approximately 2115 hours, but time of death was estimated at between 2000 hours and 2023 based on the information available at the time. I then left her with the RCMP so that they could continue their investigation on the manner and background of events that led up to the final demise of Tammy King.

It was dated September 7, 1988, then signed and witnessed, so he must have written it that same night.

It was now almost 10 p.m. John and Bob Dobbin had gone home to their families. Their roles were now completed in the drama of the life and death of Tammy King. Most of the roles played in her tragedy that night were minor.

Dr. Waldo had walked from the wharf towards his own death two years later. He too was not a major player in this tragedy. He did perform his professional duties with dispatch and effectiveness.

The RCMP soon cleared the wharf of the curious and benumbed people of Deep Harbour, who now walked around in a quiet daze. Some mulled around the wharf apron talking in hushed whispers.

The scene was cordoned off and the ambulance arrived at the wharf for the body. Before he left, Dr. Waldo had replaced the yellow tarp over Tammy's body. She lay quietly in the bottom of the boat. The ambulance drivers found her there and completed their sombre work. The ambulance lights came on as the vehicle with its cold cargo sped off into the night. The flashing, red ambulance lights splashed along the harbour road on their way to St. John's.

Near the wharf, the circling beacon of the police lights lit up the night in red, white and blue as the anonymous officer quietly completed his paperwork in the front seat of his van.

CHAPTER 2

FILE 13

My sparrow, you are not here.
The sides of wet stones cannot console me,
Nor the moss, wound with the last light.

If only I could nudge you from this sleep,
My maimed darling, my skittery pigeon.
Over this damp grave I speak the words of my love;
I, with no rights in this matter,
Neither father nor lover.

Theodore Roethke, "Elegy for Jane"

When I heard the news about Tammy's death I remembered
Dylan Thomas' poem, "A Refusal to Mourn the Death by Fire of
a Child in London", and especially Theodore Roethke's "Elegy
for Jane My Student". I tried to make sense of the senseless and
tried to explain the inexplicable. The poetry that I teach every day
showed me how these things had been dealt with by other people.

I remembered the attractive fourteen year old who had
walked into my last year's Religion 1108 class. She walked
quietly, taking little steps on her high heels. Her cosmopolitan
outfit seemed somewhat out of place in a room full of sneakered
teenagers. I remembered her white silk blouse and a little black
tie and matching black skirt. She was strikingly pretty and
dressed beyond her years.

Her face was serious for the most part which also made her seem mature. There was tasteful use of makeup especially around her big, dark eyes. She had a full mouth and cheeks that suggested a hidden mirth which rarely bobbed to the surface.

At other times that face reflected irritation at a certain boy who teased her. Sometimes he sat behind her and pulled on her blouse or brassiere strap. She would squirm and twist but never complain.

"Tammy, is he bothering you?" I asked. She said nothing.

I reprimanded him, moved him to another seat but the next day he would be back beside or behind her. I remember keeping her after school one day and saying to her, "Tammy, you have got to speak up if someone is bothering you. It makes me look like a fool if I accuse him, he denies it and you say nothing."

She said nothing once again. Perhaps she murmured a low "Yes sir," or nodded quietly.

Usually she sat in her desk with her back straight up and attentively listened to my classes. I suspect she was the same in her other classes. She was a good student who never caused trouble; she was very polite and dutiful to her studies. She was a quiet girl who did nothing to draw attention to herself except for her natural beauty and attractive clothes.

We were told at first that her death was a suicide. In my fifteen year teaching career, she was the third of my students to commit suicide.

"In loco parentis" is a Latin legal term that describes a teacher's role during the school day. It roughly translates to "in place of the parent." It refers to a teacher's legal responsibility to act as a parent would act in the same circumstances. Like a parent, a teacher feels a deep sense of loss when a student dies tragically. We, too, feel sorrow, guilt, and recognition of the horrible mortality facing our children. By extension we feel the cool draft of our own mortality.

There were so many questions. I remember asking our librarian about Tammy's parents.

"She was a foster child," I was told.

"Who did she live with?"

"Over in Deep Harbour with Albert Weller."

"How do I know that name?"

"Ann lived over there too."

"Ann Wicks? Was Ann a foster child?"

"That's a fact." The librarian was gone through the door with a box of books.

I remembered pleasant, blond-headed Ann who had left our school the year before.

With Tammy's death, a general gloom fell over the school staff of twenty seven, many of whom, like myself, had grown up in the area. I cannot say we talked about it much but somehow, for a brief time, we all felt different about our jobs, our students and perhaps our lives.

But the normal duties of opening school still confronted us: new classes, new students, new problems; ordering books, arranging seating plans, starting off the new courses, preparing lesson plans.

But, this year the burden was different. I walked as if a lead weight dragged along the floor behind me. The trek to the top floor seemed a little longer, the coolness of the basement classrooms seemed a little darker.

Some people are cynical about the old cliche that teachers mould young lives. Well, it is true, and that is why the saying has stayed around for so long. When a student dies tragically it is as if you were looking at a beautiful work of art and suddenly someone took it and smashed it at your feet.

"This bothers me like nothing else," I confided to friends John Payne and his wife, Gail, one evening at their house in Baywood.

"What do you mean?" he asked.

"Tammy's death; something about it bothers me."

"A lot about it bothers you," said Gail. "She's dead."

"No, I mean more than that."

John was standing in front of an easel where he worked on a painting taller than himself. The painting was of a huge tree which had fallen and its roots were exposed.

Bach was playing softly in the background. The room was full of plants and growing things. Down over a step was a sunroom with more plants.

Occasionally John turned around from the painting. He had steady eyes and a beard streaked with grey. He held the brush with thick fingers that seemed more like a carpenter's than an artist's. He laid the brush down on the table behind him and reached for a cigarette burning in the ash tray.

He put one hand into his thick apron and held the cigarette in the other. He stood back and appraised the work in progress.

The window behind the painting was itself a painting of early fall. The late September deciduous trees still held their leaves. But soon they too would feel the chill that I was already feeling. Their sap would sink and their leaves would dry, curl and fall to the ground. Autumn came.

Soon my mind left Tammy as I tried to relegate her to the other tragedies I had met in forty years on this planet.

The school year was passing. One of my students got pregnant, another attempted suicide, another got pregnant, another thought she was pregnant.

I came into the staff room one cold, dull day in March and heard a fellow teacher say the word "Tammy". The leaden sky loomed through the expanse of staff room windows. A lead pall went across my soul at the name. It summoned more emotion in me than I thought reasonable, since I had not heard her name for so long.

"What did you say?" I asked.

"Oh. Just about the Judicial Inquiry."

"What inquiry?"

"The inquiry into the circumstances of her death."

"When are they having it?"

"They had it. It ended last week in Baywood."

"Were you there?" I asked.

"No, I just heard about it today."

"Was there a sign on the bulletin board?"

"No. Nothing."

"Was the school invited to testify? The guidance counsellor?"

"I don't know, but I don't think so," he said.

Rumours persisted among the staff that there was more to Tammy's death than had first met the eye. One or two who had contacts with the Baywood RCMP detachment hinted at an investigation. I asked friends in the community, but information was scanty at best.

The RCMP have no real avenues of communications with the community. The Department of Justice saw no need to communicate with the citizenry, either to receive information or to give it.

Along with unofficial secrecy there was a shame in the community to discuss Tammy. Suicide was embarrassing. As well many people knew or were related to the Weller family. The Weller children came to our school as well as their foster children. There was a genuine reluctance to gossip. In a small area everybody knows about skeletons in other peoples' closets and it is unacceptable to discuss them openly. This is a reverse "Everybody knows your business" dictum that minimizes slander and gossip. There was a feeling that it was not quite christian to judge other people, to discuss their transgressions, or to cast stones.

As well, Newfoundland's Catholic communities were closing ranks on another horrible matter: The day after Tammy's body was taken from the waters of the local harbour, Father Jim Hickey pleaded guilty to twenty counts of sexual assault, indecent assault and gross indecency against boys. The whole Newfoundland Catholic community was traumatized.

Jim Hickey was up until then, arguably, the most respected of Newfoundland's priests. Editor of the Roman Catholic newspaper "The Monitor", Hickey's main ministry had been to the province's youth. He had organized a huge youth rally to welcome Prince Charles and the Lady Diana to Newfoundland. He had sat between them on the podium. On the visit to Newfoundland by Pope John Paul II, Father Hickey had again been centre stage in introducing His Holiness to dignitaries at Quidi Vidi Lake in St. John's.

The charges against Father Hickey created a turmoil of emotions among the Catholic settlements of Newfoundland. Hickey had been accepted as the best of priests. Rumours of his wrongdoing had been dismissed as malicious, and even the laying of criminal charges by the Justice Department had been questioned. Soon more rumours flew and more charges were laid against other priests and Christian Brothers. These men had been personal friends and examples of behaviour to many.

On June 28, 1989 the Royal Commission of Inquiry headed by former Ontario Chief Justice Samuel Hughes began its first televised session. The residents of St. John's could hear witnesses tell each detail of abuse by Christian Brothers and secular abusers of children. The Commission's terms of reference had been expanded by the newly-elected Liberal Government to include complaints of abuse in foster homes.

At home, the shell-shocked faithful had to survive highlights on the evening news. It was especially painful for older folks like my mother and other staunch defenders of the Church. They felt let down and embarrassed in the eyes of the protestant majority to the north and south of our Catholic enclave. Soon their shame would be shared by other faiths as the revelations of abuse spread to almost all corners of officialdom, both religious and secular.

September 1989 came and brought with it a new school year. With it as well came more horrible revelations by the Hughes Inquiry of abuse against children.

At school we were numb with the continual dosage of physical and sexual abuse and injury done to the innocent and the defenceless. Almost all the victims were children and orphans used for the emotional and sexual pleasures of adults in whose custody they had been placed.

Our students heard the same litanies of abuse by superiors as we heard every evening. They knew that priests, brothers, and some teachers had already been charged. We saw the distrust for all authority grow in their eyes. The respect for the church and the good it could do was lost in many of them. There was much negative generalization about the clergy.

The institutions of authority and morality in our lives were being discredited before our eyes. As the Hughes Inquiry unfolded it seemed that society's foundations - Justice, Social Services, Church - were involved with abuse, neglect or cover-up. It was horrible.

It was not a good time to be teaching religion in a Catholic school. Or perhaps it was. I remember some of the frankest classroom discussions I ever had with students during this period. Often their reaction was anger and condemnation. They had been hurt and betrayed. Only the classroom cynics were left unscathed, pruning themselves like wise old cats in their wisdom.

John Payne and Gail were my confidants during this time. Payne, a protestant, had a fascination for all things Roman Catholic. Many of his paintings reflected this Catholic spirituality. He had painted a huge Easter triptych with Christ crucified on a spruce cross over the Ferryland Downs.

I remembered the third part of the triptych: The risen Christ floats over the waters of the cold Atlantic instead of the warm azure of his native Mediterranean. Behind him three Newfoundland fishermen haul a net into a dory. His white raiment contains and exudes a bright light of hope and grace for even the commonest creature.

One evening in early spring of 1990 I visited Payne.

"Still thinking about Tammy King?" he asked.

"Of course."

"There's more to it than a suicide, you know."

"What do you mean?"

"The RCMP have already done an investigation."

"How do you know?"

"I have my sources. Her foster father, Albert Weller, has been accused of sexual assault by another girl. Someone named Ann Wicks."

"Ann!" I couldn't believe what I was hearing.

"Did you know her?"

"Of course. She was a student of mine. She lived in the same foster home!"

"Well you knew them both. Maybe you should write something about it."

I mulled over his revelations as I drove home that spring evening. It was mind boggling: Tammy dead and Ann a victim of sexual assault?

I remembered back to the past year. I had conducted an anonymous survey on various kinds of abuse with my religion classes. Tammy had been one of my students. It had been a very simple questionnaire with three or four questions, one of which was: "Have you ever been sexually abused?"

I had explained to the three high school classes that sexual abuse was a problem on the increase and we should know if it was a problem at our school. I had explained that their answers to the questionnaire would be totally confidential. Even I would never know who said yes and who said no. No names were given or requested. I just wanted to know if we had a problem. Each student had taken a questionnaire, gone to another room, marked an "X" for the correct answers, returned and dropped the folded questionnaire in my desk drawer.

I remembered having gone to my principal, a member of the Order of Irish Christian Brothers, with the statistics from my survey. Besides showing that 6% of the grade ten students were being sexually abused, it showed that 33% of them already had their first sexual experience and that a number were being physically abused. It also showed that the figures were higher for the grade twelve students. The grade elevens had decided not to participate in the survey.

In his office he had listened to what I had said.

"I think we have a problem, Brother, especially with sexual abuse and sexual activity."

"Are you sure your results are reliable?"

"Yes, Brother, I am."

"Mr. Moore, we must always remember that we teach in a Catholic school." Then he had looked up from where he sat at his desk and held my eye. The conversation had terminated.

My classes had to stay within the teachings of the church. This had implications about what I could teach regarding human sexuality, birth control, AIDS education, etc.

In Newfoundland we have a church run or denominational school system. There is no alternative public school system. We are the only province in Canada, in fact the only educational jurisdiction on the continent like it.

About a week after my chat with the principal about my survey, I had been on lunch supervision in the cafeteria. He had come up to me and said:

"There have been some complaints about your surveys."

"What do you mean, Brother?"

"Rumours are being spread about which girls are sexually

active, which girls are pregnant, that sort of thing."

"Are you serious?"

"I surely am serious. It's very upsetting to these girls in question."

"Yes, I can imagine."

"I think you should stop talking about your surveys until things cool down."

I had not pursued it any further that year. I had reasoned that I had informed my superiors. But I felt confused that the students, whom I had set out to help, had been hurt by the process. I felt as well that I had been reprimanded.

Thus the secrecy continued to thrive even in my own little world, in spite of my naive attempts to explore it. I had yet to understand this "ogre in the fog," secrecy, and how it is an essential part of sexual abuse. I had yet to learn of the ogre of secrecy's many guises, and uses of well-meaning people, to protect one of its fetid treasures, sexual abuse.

A year later, on that Spring day in 1990, when I arrived home from John Payne's house, I went through my old filing cabinet to find the survey results for Tammy's class. To my surprise the completed questionnaires were still there. I took out the folder for her class; Religion 1108, 1988. I went through the questionnaires with the "X"s showing who had been free of the purges of abuse. Then I came to the first "X" by the "YES" to sexual abuse. Then I came to the second. There were no more.

I put the two anonymous questionnaires side by side on the desk in front of me. My mind reeled. In all probability Tammy had written one of them. This was the closest she had ever come to telling someone in authority about the sexual abuse. It had been only months before she died. I looked at the two mute sheets of paper - two silent documents of abuse, secrecy and shame. In Tammy's case I had stumbled close to the truth. But the ogre of secrecy had again triumphed.

In retrospect, there were a number of things we could have done when we knew that students in that class were being sexually abused six months before Tammy's death.

The two questionnaires on my desk lay silent through my reverie. I knew the statistics from the USA that said one in four girls were sexually abused by the time they reached eighteen. The "Badgley Report" in Canada had put the figures much higher. But somehow I felt that these statistics did not apply to the girls under my care and control in Newfoundland schools.

My students had never spoken of abuse. *They did not look abused.* They sat in my room and looked back at me from their desks while I told them about Jesus cursing the fig tree. In Literature class we watched and discussed Polanski's "Macbeth" and Zeferelli's "Romeo and Juliet".

I looked at the questionnaire on the left. It may have been Tammy's. She had reached her hand out only this far for help. She knew I was concerned, why did she not tell me about the abuse? Why did she not ask for help? She must have known that I and others would have been more than willing to give that help and stop the sexual abuse. I had much to learn about the ogre of secrecy.

One night I mentioned it at John Payne's house.

"So there were two questionnaires with "yes" to the sexual abuse question," he mused.

"What do you mean?"

"Well, if Tammy was one of them, who was the second?"

The thought shook me. It had never occurred to me to consider the second student. I looked at Payne silently as he followed his thoughts further.

"There is another kid from that same class out there who was also being abused, and may still be." He waved his hand in front of him towards the large patio doors that led out into the dark.

"The second one," I thought aloud.

"There are probably more kids out there tonight who are being abused."

Outside, a single star peeped through the tall dark poplars beyond his deck. I followed him out through the patio doors. It was a perfect spring night in 1990. The deciduous trees that surround his house were once again full of foliage. They moved full and restless in the evening breeze. It was still cool but the air was clear and over the tops of the poplars I could now see that instead of one lone star, a dozen constellations blinked and beckoned at me from a black sky.

"It has all the elements of pure tragedy, Tom. You should

write about it."

"I don't know anything about sexual abuse."

"Well, you should find out."

"How? I'm a school teacher not an investigator."

"But do you want to?"

"More than anything." I was surprised to hear myself say.

"There is someone you should meet."

"OK. Who?"

"Clitus Rowe."

The name was vaguely familiar. "Right. Who is Clitus Rowe?"

"Clitus Rowe is a lawyer from Ontario. He's in Newfoundland as a counsel for the Hughes Commission."

"So how can he help me?"

"He is handling the investigation of Tammy's death and abuse."

"What? Is she being investigated by the Hughes Commission?"

"Absolutely."

"I thought that the Hughes Commission only dealt with orphans from Mount Cashel."

"The provincial government has widened their scope to include foster homes. You should meet Clitus."

"How did you meet him?"

"He bought one of my paintings. He's a good guy."

"With real good taste in art? Right?"

"Meet him."

I said nothing.

So far I had invested little of myself in Tammy's story. A little maudlin sentimentality, a few tears for a dead student. Now I was being challenged to go deeper, to invest time, emotion, myself. Like the cat in the adage, I hesitated on the edge of the sea.

A week later, on June 15th, 1990 I arrived at John's house with a bottle of Scotch to meet Clitus Rowe. It was the first hot, sunny day that summer. Gail was reading in the cool of the studio, lost in a sea of her green plants. She looked like a girl of sixteen as she lay on their old sofa with one leg hooked up over the back.

"What are you reading?"

"Hi Tom," came a cheery greeting. "Oh, this? It's the Tao Te Ching."

"Any good?"

"It's wonderful. It's by a Chinese philosopher Lao-Tzu. He was a contemporary of Confucius."

Behind her was the painting John was working on. There was a huge rock on a wind swept barren. On one side of the rock was open sea and a wind coming off the water. Behind the rock crouched a woman with a baby in her arms.

"It's called 'Mother and Child', she said noticing my gaze.

"It's beautiful."

"He's still working on it." She laid down her book and swung her feet to the floor to better see the painting.

The mother looked behind her in trepidation as she clutched the infant to her breast. The child was covered in a cloak that seemed to meld it to her body. The painting was full of tension, fear and foreboding. A Madonna and Child set on a Newfoundland barren.

"Clitus Rowe is already here; he and John are out on the deck." She swung back up to the sofa and grabbed up her book. I left her with Lao-Tzu.

John welcomed me and introduced me to the man sitting with him on the sunny deck.

"Tom, meet Clitus Rowe."

A short, pleasant man of about forty-five or fifty rose to shake my hand. Clitus Rowe was compact and wiry. The hair was greyed and thinning. But the lightness of step and movement suggested a man whose energies had declined from phenomenal to merely great. He possessed a natural self-deprecation which is impossible to imitate. It is so refreshing and rare in people in authority and so boring in those who are not.

"Mr. Rowe, nice to meet you."

"Tom is a writer," said John.

"How did you two meet?" Clitus asked.

"I remember driving down to the Southern Shore to meet the guy who was going to paint the cover of my book."

"You wanted to check him out first?" Clitus ventured with a laugh. "John says you want to write a book about Tammy King."

"I want to find out what happened to her. Maybe I'll write something. I am hearing lots of rumours but there is so little real information. "

"There is now," Clitus said.

"What do you mean?"

"How would you like access to RCMP files, Justice Department files, Social Services files, autopsy reports, Judicial Inquiry report, and coroner, forensic, and medical reports?"

"Are these available?"

"With a Royal Commission those documents are subpoenaed and available to the public."

"You mean I can get copies?"

"The copy given to you will have the names deleted, everything else would be there."

"I already know most of the names."

He placed a white plastic binder on the table in front of me. He leaned back in his chair and rolled down his shirt collar to get the most of the sun.

I remember this day as the first day of real summer that year, 1990. The hot sun of that day, so early for a Newfoundland summer, was soon replaced by our usual spring rain, drizzle and fog. For me it was the first day of a search that was to possess me for four years.

The sun was shining hot on the three of us on the deck. The plastic cover was soft in the heat as I held the thick document in my hand. At the top of the cover read, "Royal Commission of Inquiry Into the Response of the Newfoundland Criminal Justice System to Complaints". Mid way down the page read in block capitals:

CHILD WELFARE/CRIMINAL INVESTIGATION
PROFILES:
NO 13
1986 TO 1990

This was Tammy's file dated May, 17, 1990, one month earlier. It took me half an hour to scan the document. The bound sheets comprised just under two hundred pages. It included files from the RCMP, Provincial Justice Department and Provincial Social Services.

Page (i) reads:
"The files indicate the following areas of concern:

1.   the degree of responsibility to report an allegation of abuse to the Director of Child Welfare when the alleged victim is now an adult but the alleged abuse takes place in a foster home which continues to care for children who are the responsibility of the Director of Child Welfare;

2.   the response by the Department of Social Services to prior allegation of abuse when children still reside in the home of foster parents where that prior abuse is alleged to have taken place;

3.   the timeliness of the response by police who have been advised of the alleged sexual abuse which has taken place in the past but relates to a foster home where other children are currently in care."

"What do you think, Tom?" Payne asked.

"At least now there's information about her death. A pity it took a judge from Ontario to compile it and a lawyer from Ontario to release it," I murmured aloud.

Clitus took no offense."You'll need time to go through the files, the RCMP files are interesting."

"What do you mean, interesting?"

"The RCMP knew that Weller had sexually assaulted another girl twenty days before they even went to the house."

"You mean they left Tammy there with Weller?" John asked.

"Tammy and her younger sister, Maggie. Social Services knew about it even earlier."

"They too left the girls in the house for almost three weeks?"

"More than three weeks!" Clitus nodded his head, took a deep sip of his whisky. He slumped down in his chair and looked at me through the tops of his glasses with his chin on his chest.

I looked at her pictures so eloquent in death. They spoke of a young and dependent victim. The pale lips spoke no words of explanation. The cold bruised limbs indicated no direction nor pointed a finger of guilt. Many questions leaped across my mind but no answers followed them.

"The whole thing seems so unfair," John was talking.

We both nodded. "I see it every day at the Hughes Inquiry," Clitus went on. "I have never seen anything sadder or more unfair than what was done to these children. They were defenceless, no family present, no one to take their part."

So we sat on John's deck on that first hot day of summer, 1990. We talked about Tammy King. I learned much about the case and on that deck I began my search to put together the life of that unfortunate young girl. The secrecy taunted me and I wanted to know. Then I wanted to tell people who cared.

Too soon Clitus rose. "Well folks I have to get back to St. John's. We're still very much in the middle of this thing."

"I don't envy you your job," John said.

"No. I'd much rather stay out here and paint pictures. But I have no talent." He laughed.

I couldn't help but think how valuable a talent the man did have and how desperately it was needed by the children of Newfoundland.

"Tom, my office is at Exon House. Come in and we'll get you a copy of file 13. That is a good place to start. It contains all the information we were able to gather."

"Thank's, Clitus, I think I will."

And so I did. When my summer holidays arrived a week or two later, I went to Exon House to meet with Clitus Rowe and view the Royal Commission at work. I met David Day, Herb Vivien and the other tireless workers on the Hughes Commission of Inquiry.

The hearings began at the former Exon House in St. John's September 11, 1989. Perhaps it is a poignant irony that the building had formerly housed crippled and handicapped children. Their silent echoes and ghostly rumblings reminded everyone who entered of the need for justice for their injured fellows.

The hearings continued until June 29, 1990. They were recorded by Avalon Cablevision of St. John's on the understanding that the company could rebroadcast them later. This saved the commission scarce dollars, provided a reliable record of what was said for future reference, and made the hearings truly public.

The ogre of secrecy had rumbled and grumbled. He had assumed the form of defender of public taste. He had exuded modesty and politely whispered to us about decorum and propriety. He said that these abusers and their crimes should not be on television assaulting the ears of young children. He had called it sensationalizing and objected to such scandalous enjoyments being offered to the soap opera crowd every afternoon.

But the truth was heard. In Exon House, the Royal Commission of Justice Samuel Hughes sat each day and heard of stories of abuse and tragedy. Hughes sat immutable, hearing the testimony of young lives ruined, the tragedy and the travesty. Often a monotoned question from the old chief justice would make a child take heart or a bureaucrat squirm.

The master of monotone was the Commission Co-Counsel, Newfoundland lawyer, David Day. His towering, slouching figure and droopy moustache served well to lull his witnesses into complacency. His copious intellect allowed witnesses long ropes of digression before yanking them back into responsibility for neglects or omissions often ten or fifteen years before.

I sat in the room where Justice Hughes heard the witnesses. His large, bald, bullet-like head looked down at the transcripts on the high desk in front of him. From time to time he would change position in his large chair, lean back and look at the witness.

If he failed to hear correctly, which was more than once, he stopped the witness with a slow clearing of his throat and a slowly worded question. He was like an old sea lion laboriously changing position in his chair.

With a plodding sense of decency, he directed the assembled human sections of the inquiry before him like an old conductor handling an orchestra: the virtuosos like Clitus Rowe and David

Day and the wind sections from the civil service and the Department of Justice, with their convenient lapses in memory.

Hughes encouraged without gullibility the painful stories of the boys and girls who testified. Many were now grown men and women, describing how their childhood had been stolen from them by their guardians and protectors. Many spoke through tears as painful memories were relived in the telling. Horrors, parts of their lives too painful to think about, long since frozen in their subconscious storehouse, were thawed out and hurt them once again.

I sat in the small auditorium at Exon house and listened to the testimony. One voice spoke at a time in a quiet room. It was something like a courtroom scene on TV. But unlike TV, there was no background music to coach our emotions to a crescendo. There were no jangled discords to prompt our ears to the unspeakable horrors. Each horror was spoken in halting but clear English in front of the Commissioner, several dozen other people and a TV camera.

The jaded young camera man yawned from time to time and looked around the room. But his machine did not. The single eye of the lens, like the eye of God, never wavered from the witness. every question, answer, sob and sigh was recorded for broadcast and future examination. I later viewed many of the tapes in my search.

One such tape showed Day interviewing Frank Simms, the Director of Child Welfare from 1971 to 1989. It was during his tenure as chief custodian of the foster children of Newfoundland that the tragedies at Deep Harbour and Mount Cashel occurred. In the latter young boys were abused for years by Christian Brothers and by older boys. The young victims, in turn, became abusers who tormented the next generation of boys in the orphanage.

I remember David Day trying to locate a document written by Simms about a visit by Chesley Riche to Simms' office on December 8, 1975. Chesley Rich claimed to have warned Simms of the abuse at that meeting.

Riche was an unemployed volunteer maintenance man at Mount Cashel orphanage for boys. He had been appalled at the physical and sexual abuse he had witnessed there. Directed by a good heart and not by section 49 of the Child Welfare Act of Newfoundland, Chesley Riche had reported the matter to the Director of Child Welfare, Frank Simms. He had graphically described the abuse and named the boys being victimized. But Chesley Riche had underestimated the ogre of secrecy.

Fifteen years later, when the abuse finally became public knowledge, Simms had difficulty remembering the meeting. He also had difficulty remembering what had happened to his written record of that meeting. The record had mysteriously disappeared from the file. The document would be essential in establishing what action Simms had taken or neglected to take.

Day, the droopy hound with the keen nose droned on:

DAY: Mr Simms, having had this meeting with Chesley Riche, did you at that point in time write down either on a scrap of paper in a memo pad or in some other more formal writing, particulars of Mr. Riche's complaints and either attach them to a file or sent your notes out to be attached to a new file within headquarters?

SIMMS: Well, sir, I have not had the opportunity to examine the official file because it has not been available to me. So I can't tell you that there's anything there or not. Normally something would have been written and placed into a file....Whether it was done or whether it exists now, I'm sorry, I can't advise you of that, sir. I don't know....

DAY: ... And you say because you have not had access to the official file - I gather you are referring to the file or files relating to the Earle family that were maintained at headquarters.

SIMMS: And the Mount Cashel file.

DAY: And the Mount Cashel file. But if a written record had been made ...when I say written, typed, printed, written, shorthand for that matter, it would be either in the Mount Cashel file at headquarters, or it would be in the Earle family file at headquarters.

SIMMS: Or it may have gotten destroyed through some weeding process of the files ...of the records.

DAY: And how frequently during the period you were Director was your part of the Department given to weeding files involving child protection of the institutions and homes in which foster children under your care were living?

SIMMS: There is a record at the Department that would give you information regarding the weeding process, Mr. Day, and weeding did take place at certain times to make space for other records. Space was at a premium and weeding had to take place, sir.

Later, after the recess, Day droned on again:

DAY: ... Is it a fact that prior to your leaving office as Director of Child Welfare on 31 March, 1989, you requested from your staff and received and examined and then returned the Mount Cashel headquarters file, the Earle Social Services' file as well as other files that were maintained at headquarters office at that time?

SIMMS: I don't recall asking for the Earle file. I recall asking for all files relating to Mount Cashel. That's the way that I remember it, sir, and I may have seen the Earle file, but I don't recall requesting it....I was asked to prepare a statement for the Royal Newfoundland Constabulary, and I asked for the records to refresh my memory.

Other questions provided a variation of the main theme to which Day sooner of later returned:

DAY: ... If a record were made of your telephone conversation or of your meeting with Chesley Riche, if it were made and if it were placed in one of what you recall as being four Mount Cashel files, and if it isn't there now in one of those four files, of your understanding, how many different explanations might be available for it not being there, other than weeding?

SIMMS: There is no other, Mr.Day, that I can think of unless it ...if it was loose and accidentally dropped out of the file.

DAY: ... But the likelihood is that you did make some note or record.

SIMMS: After 14 years, Mr.Day, the honesty of it, sir, is I cannot remember.

DAY: So that to summarize your evidence to this point in relation to documentation, I take it that there are now three possible reasons no record of your meeting with Mr. Riche has surfaced, at least within the knowledge of our Commission. One, if it were a loose piece of paper rather than part of a running record that would be affixed to the file, it could have fallen out of the file. Secondly, the record could have left the file through the weeding policy established by the administrative branch of the Department of Social Services, and thirdly, no record was made so there was none to be weeded and none to be lost. Fair statement?

SIMMS: Uh-hum.

Later, an impatient Commissioner Hughes interrupted the exchange:

HUGHES: Mr. Simms, you say that you do remember discussing or sharing it with the Assistant Director, and you say that you do remember meeting with the Assistant Deputy Minister, and then you say "I would have told them." Now if you remember meeting with them on this occasion can you not say you remember telling them?

SIMMS: Mr. Commissioner, it would be extremely difficult for me to remember exactly what I shared with them, sir.

Later still, Hughes lost patience with the bureaucrat:

SIMMS: But I think there is a situation that ought to be brought into this day, Mr.Day...

HUGHES: The only situation that should be brought in right now if you please, Mr. Simms, is to listen to counsel's question and endeavour to answer it, not to meet it with another statement. Could you put the question again please, Mr. Day.

How did Tammy die? Why did she die? How did a little girl born into the peace and security of a western democracy decide, at fifteen, that life was hopeless and not worth living?

That was what I resolved to discover. I was to have a number of my polite assumptions stripped away; about good and evil, about our society and its care for its disadvantaged, and about the nature of sexual abuse. I was to learn about the ogre of secrecy and his many disguises.

I was not always ready to handle the truth my search exposed. My preconceptions were so much easier, nicer, neater. I followed the journey of her short life down many paths from her birth place near the cliffs of St. John's to the overgrown path to her final cliff in Deep Harbour. This book is a record of that journey.

CHAPTER 3

ST. JOHN'S NEWFOUNDLAND

Just as the twig is bent, the tree is inclined.

Alexander Pope

The day that Tammy was born, November 9, 1972, was cold, overcast and wet in St. John's, Newfoundland. The temperatures ranged between 4 and 7 degrees Celsius, making it an uncomfortable but not unseasonable day for that time of year. It was the first of three days of rain that steadily increased until on the third day, three inches of rain fell on the city. A brisk northeast wind brought the rain in from the wide expanse of North Atlantic that stretched unbroken by land for 5000 kilometers to Ireland. In 1972 St. John's was the rainiest, foggiest, windiest and poorest city in Canada; with the highest unemployment, the highest taxes, the lowest per capita income in the nation.

It still is.

In the early afternoon of November 9, Katie King knew her baby was coming soon. She and her husband, Tom lived on Long's Hill in a section of row housing. Their narrow, three-story, charcoal-grey house was the end unit on the right, half way down the hill. It was attached on the upper side to a half dozen similar dwellings.

Their house was physically dreary and sparsely furnished. It was neither a warm nor pleasant place to bring home a little baby in November. Their only heat was the cooking stove in the basement kitchen. They had a TV but were without a washing machine. Katie washed the family clothes by hand.

From their top floor window Katie could look down Long's Hill in the direction of the harbour. There were two bedrooms on the top floor, the ground floor entrance led to a porch and living room and the kitchen was downstairs in the basement. She remembers the house was "like a lighthouse", narrow and tall.

"The welfare could have given me better. I never had hot and cold water. I used to wash the baby's clothes in a tub with a washing board. Then walk up to the top floor where I had a line to dry them. Once I fell down all the stairs and my sister was there. She thought I was killed."

The previous tenant had been a prostitute who had enjoyed a brisk trade before moving on for reasons unknown.

Before her, the premises had been rented by a lonely gentleman who spent long evenings standing in the upstairs window smoking a cigar as he gazed down the street.

The landlord was a man named Dick Aspel, who looked after all the houses in the row and collected rents for the absent owner. In the case of Tom and Katie King, as with many tenants on that hill, the rent was paid directly by the Department of Social Services to the landlord.

The Kings did not own a car, so when she felt her time was due, Tom's brother Peter drove Katie to the Grace General Hospital. The hospital, run by the Salvation Army, was on Lemarchant Road about ten minutes away. With her labour pains already beginning, Katie looked out at an overcast St. John's sky as a nervous brother-in-law sped towards the hospital.

Katie did not even make it to the delivery room. The baby, eager to get into this world, had to be delivered by a nurse on the ward. Eighteen years later, Katie recalled:

> Tammy was born about 2:30 at the Grace Hospital. She was a big chubby baby, nine pounds and fourteen ounces. It was a fast delivery. The girl on the floor borned her. I couldn't go to the operating room. I borned her too fast.

> It had been a beautiful pregnancy, a beautiful birth, a beautiful girl. They wrapped her up and brought her to my room the next morning. They said, 'There's your little girl.' And what a beauty! Right coal black hair, brown eyes. My heart went out to her and I held her. I gave her a bottle, which is natural and I couldn't wait to get her home.

Hospital records show a smaller birth weight than Katie recalled: seven pounds, six and three-quarter ounces. Other than that, "Baby King" was born much as her mother remembered at 2:03 p.m. on November 9, 1972.

On November 13th Katie was discharged from "the Grace" and brought the new baby to their home on Long's Hill.

In 1972 the appropriately-named hill was one of the main thoroughfares to and from the Water Street and downtown areas. Before the plethora of shopping malls, downtown had been the commercial heart of the city. The "west loop bus" came up Long's Hill.

"The kids used to play on the sidewalk in front of their houses," as one resident puts it, "Long's Hill had once been a growing, if not prosperous, part of the city. But in the 1950's and early 1960's it became a low socio-economic area."

Tammy was the third child living with Tom and Katie: There was a daughter, Bonny, who was three, and a son, Tommy, who was two. Katie had another daughter, April, who had been given up for adoption some years before. Since she married Tom, there had been a boy, Gary, who had also been put up for adoption. Katie had lost a baby some months before Tammy was conceived. Other children, Maggie and Liza, were soon to follow.

Katie King's memories of those days, for the most part, appear to be pleasant:

> When Tammy went to school on the first day she was frightened and she cried. She came back and said, 'Mom, I don't like school.' 'You'll like it tomorrow,' I said. She came back the next day and said can I put a

little outfit on her, tunic and blouse and all this stuff, so she could be like the other girls.

I dressed her up beautiful. She went to school and she loved it. She went to the Kirk, right here on Long's Hill. After that she went to Harrington Elementary with her sister Bonny and her brother Tommy. They were doing fine, three of them in school. I had another daughter, Maggie. Maggie clung with Tammy. Always together. I had Maggie after I had Tammy. They still are close together, as far as I'm concerned. They're sisters.

She wanted to become somebody. She wanted to accomplish something. All together I had seven children. Tammy was my favourite because she would always bring me these little "Morning Glories" after school. Anything would please her. Tammy never complained. Only when she had the tonsils.

I brought her down to the Janeway Hospital. They were beautiful. They helped her. She must have been seven. The doctor said she could not have her tonsils removed till she was in her teens. In the night time I would sing to her, to control the tonsils I'd sing to her. I'd tell her little stories. She'd be interested in that and she wouldn't cry if I'd say, 'don't cry, Tammy.' It would take the hurt away. (Katie cries).

Very agreeable child, but sometimes too trusting. She'd never complain. It was once she complained to me about a girl was hitting at her, another girl in school. And she hated doing that. She said, 'Mommy, this girl is tormenting me.'

I said, 'Who is she?'

I had a little talk with her and her mother.

Tammy never went out late, she never smoked marijuana, she never drank, she never done anything else. She'd be in just after school and then she'd go to church. Down at the Salvation Army she'd go and she'd always sing this song to me: 'God loves you and I love you and that's the way it should be.'

She was too trusting towards people and liking them too much, trying to get ahead in life, looking after herself. She wanted to be someone.

Life on Long's Hill was difficult for Tom and Katie and for their children. Tom had not held a job for years and Katie too did not work. Their lives were sustained by the Department of Social Services.

There was a considerable amount of drinking going on in the home. Tom and Katie drank heavily whenever their finances would allow and sometimes when they would not. There was often a boarder who drank with them. Katie's two brothers, Frankie and Walter Tucker, spent a lot of time at the house. The main activity on these occasions was drinking. Both young men subsequently died in alcohol-related incidents while still in their thirties.

Alcohol had played a major role in Tom King's life for some time. His mother and father had been heavy drinkers. His father was Tom King Sr., a city council worker who had gone overseas with the Canadian Army during the war. A serious man with dark good looks, Tom Sr. was fifteen years older than Tom's mother, Molly King. She was visually impaired.

Tom's brother, Peter, remembered their father:

My father was married a couple of times and my mother was married once before. In our family there was seven: three boys and four girls, and I'm the second oldest. My brother Tom, Tammy's father was the oldest. He was born October 23, 1947 when Mom lived on Prospect Street down in the older part of St. John's. She later moved to Springdale Street.

We came from a poor family, sort of a welfare family in the sense that my father never lived with my mother completely. He would spend week-ends, and he was there half the time, sort of a haphazard relationship. They were never really married but they lived together as man and wife for twenty-seven years, until she died.

Dad (Tom Senior) worked all his life. He worked at city council as a maintenance worker and a construction worker. Then he went overseas with, I think it was with the 159 Regiment, I think. He came back and went to work at the council and he worked there right up till the mid-sixties. He worked as a brick layer and a cement finisher off and on until he couldn't no more when he was too old, in his seventies. He used to give Mom maintenance payments along with the welfare she used to get for us.

I know she loved us, because in our house there was only a mother and no father. There wasn't a good family environment. She was handicapped because of her blindness. I wouldn't say that it was a loving environment. I know she did love us because she did it all on her own.

I remember we got put out of our house on Springdale Street because the landlord wanted to sell it. This was in 1954. Tom was 7, I was 5 and Liz was 2 or 3. We went down to St. Phillips back in the early 1950's when there was no electricity or lights or anything and Mom, half blind. She fought to do everything to get us out of there. The only way she could get us out of there was to abandon us. She walked to St. John's and went to Social Services and got us into the orphanage run by the United Church.

I remember little things about the orphanage, like the stuff they used to put in you hair for the boogies, and it used to burn like hell. I mean, they were good to us there, and clean and the food was good. I remember the place was run by a woman called Audrey. We were only there for a month. Oh, yeah, we ran away.

The three children, the oldest of whom was seven, ran away from the orphanage and found their mother. She had secured what was called a "widow's home" in Westmount, a block of welfare apartments in St. John's surrounded by Vimy, Vickers and Cashin Avenues, and Froude Avenue. It was in a neighbourhood called Mundy Pond.

There were roughly seventeen blocks with four apartments in each one: two up and two down. The basement was for the coal pounds, everybody burned coal then. The cement blocks to build Westmount came from the American base at Pleasantville. It was low income housing built by the government.

Tammy's grandfather, Tom Sr. acknowledged all Molly King's children as his own, but he lived with his aging mother until her death in 1964. Then he and Molly lived together until her death in July, 1977.

By 1964 Tammy's father, Tom, and younger brothers Peter and Bob were all into their teen years and beyond the correction of Tom King Sr. and half-blind Molly. Tom was Roman Catholic and a strict man about some things, like cursing and taking the Lord's name. His fondness for drinking tended to undermine any advice or example he might have given to his sons and daughters. His example of hard work was passed on to son Peter who earned for himself a good wife, family, job, and a happy home. But even this example was soon to be lost on Tom.

None of the children were raised Catholic. All survived what could be understated as "difficult" childhoods.

Tammy's Uncle Peter recalled his own rough childhood:

> Through our pre-teen and teenage years we were living in Westmount. That was a very poor and hard part of St. John's. We were part of the welfare families; we got notes to go to school to get our books. We got clothes from the churches as hand outs to wear because the welfare didn't give you too much then.

> Mom drank too. Not as much as Dad but that was because she had all of us to care for. But she did like a drink. She got a couple of bucks on the weekend and that was it. Years ago, before Dad moved in, she'd get a bottle of wine and drink it with her father. He used to stay with us before Dad moved in 1964. They weren't drunk all the time or anything like that. But I'd say, on weekends they were pretty well drunk.

> Dad was probably gone to Baywood with his friends and Mom would be home with us. But there was always grub and good hearty meals, like "Jigs Dinner", fish and

brewis and meat and potatoes. Usually with that much alcohol involved, you're usually eating out of a can.

After so many years her drinking progressed and Dad too drank more because he was no longer working and he had a good pension coming in. He had a pension from the Council and a pension as a War Veteran. And she was getting a pension from the CNIB because my mother was legally blind.

The world that Tammy's father, Tom, grew up in was confusing and without clear direction. In the absence of a satisfactory family life, the boys turned more and more to the relief of alcohol. It was a well-tried remedy in the world that they knew.

As the oldest, Tom would have to look out for his siblings. Peter, two years his junior, would follow him everywhere. Often Tom would tire of this and try to rid himself of the trailing brother, to no avail. Peter says,

> I used to bug him to death because I would never let him go alone. I used to hang on to Tom like nothing else. We were close, yes. I depended upon him a lot. We went to school together, we went "on the pip" together, we went out and got into trouble together, we went to the boys home together, we got out of it together, went to jail on the mainland together.

> Tammy's father, Tom, was passive, quiet. I was always the agitator. I used to get Tom into trouble. I used to convince Tom to come an do a break and entry with me or to stay off school or to rob cheques. Tom would sign them because he was a neat writer, he had two years education on us.

55

I had the nerve. I used to go and take cheques out of the mailboxes and Tom would go and sign them. We would get another guy to go and cash them. That guy didn't have too much sense at all.We used to have a note saying that Mommy wants a block of butter, a pound of bologna, a pack of tea bags, and they'd cash the baby bonus cheques like nothing else. Tom got into a lot of trouble but he was never a violent or a physical person. As a teenager he was always quiet and likeable. Everybody liked him.

Tom looked a lot like Dad. Dad was dark and distinguished looking and at eighty he was still a good-looking man. Tom was slim, strong and good looking, even in the shabby old clothes that we had.

Molly King's children attended Springdale Street school. Study habits were not a priority at home and six or seven energetic and clever children were often more than a visually impaired Molly could handle. Scholastic success was not a priority, but regular school attendance was.

The legislation of Newfoundland requires children under the age of sixteen to attend school as a prerequisite for receiving children's allowance. For the boys, even their attendance records were less than adequate and often their mother's support from the government was docked because of their truancy. Livid protests at home did little to change the pattern.

Their truancy soon became a matter for the authorities. Their days as wayward children ended for the King brothers on August 2nd, 1962 in the Correctional Institute for Boys in Whitbourne. They were kept in the Boys' Home for two years.

In the fall of 1964 the boys were placed in a foster home in Topsail, not far from St. John's. They shared a room and stayed very close; Tom was now seventeen and Peter fifteen.

Still required to attend school, Tom was sent to grade nine at

Queen Elizabeth II High School in Foxtrap while Peter attended grade seven classes at St. John the Baptist in Topsail.

Tom soon developed an interest in a girl back in St. John's. He quit his academic career mid-way through grade nine. He left the foster home and went back to live in Westmount with his mother and father. Tom King Senior and Molly had been living together for almost a year.

Peter would have gone with him except that he was obliged to remain in school until his sixteenth birthday.

Tom King got a job at the local A&W restaurant which paid seventy cents an hour. He used to bring hamburgers home to the family after his shift which ended late at night. His mother, Molly, would iron his uniform in spite of her visual problems. There seemed to be a peaceful co-existence at Westmount as long as Tom was working. His drinking was not yet a serious problem. He had a steady girl friend, Betty, and he had a job. As events would later prove, Tom's life had peaked at seventeen.

Tom may have settled into this routine for some time except for the intervention of two people: his girl friend's mother, and Peter. Peter was getting restless out in the bay. Always the agitator, he had a better idea for himself and Tom. The Mainland of Canada beckoned: plenty of jobs, lots of money, plenty of girls. All they needed was a little "seed funding".

No problem! Peter arranged financing for the project. It came in the person of another friend, Phil Cross, who had grown up at Mount Cashel. Phil was working on a farm out in Topsail near Peter's foster home. Phil owned an old Harley Davidson motorcycle. Peter persuaded Phil to accompany them to Toronto and to sell his bike to finance their trip.

Tom's romance had hit a rocky stretch in the person of Betty's mother. Tom had gotten Betty pregnant and the mother shuddered at the prospect of a lifetime union of Betty and Tom. The daughter was cautioned to break off the relationship and she did.

Tom was broken hearted and susceptible to younger brother Peter's prompting to seek greener pastures beyond the Gulf of St. Lawrence.

They left St. John's on the "Newfie Bullet," a venerable,

narrow-gauge train, in the summer of 1965. Peter had waited until summer holidays in order to shake the school authorities. Off they chugged to seek their fortunes on "the Mainland" - land of dreams. It cost them thirty-five dollars each on a "red day" - the cheapest rate charged by the CNR to travel from St. John's to Toronto.

"The Mainland" did not turn out to be the nirvana promised by Peter to his fellow pilgrims. They spent a lot of time waiting around the Industrial Overload office drinking coffee and eating doughnuts. They unloaded trucks and boxcars and received their pay at the end of each day. They would then "have a scoff" and sleep at the Salvation Army hostel for fifty cents per night.

It didn't take long for the boys to get to know one of the many social strata in the city of Toronto, to meet the girls and the bars. Soon they tired of working and went to the missions where the food was free. When they had no money they would go to work for a few days to finance their eating and drinking.

It soon became mainly drinking. Living in flop houses, they drank themselves into oblivion on whatever liquid of alcoholic content available. They were arrested for common drunkenness, being drunk and disorderly, and were in jail a number of times.

Tom returned to Newfoundland after a year, in 1966, and his brother soon followed. When Peter arrived in St. John's in 1967, with his "Mainland Experience" forever behind him, Tom had already met Katie.

Katie Tucker was a vivacious teenager from an area of St. John's called Shea Heights. A lively girl, she liked to sing along with songs on the radio hit parade, and she had a keen sense of fun. Katie remembered:

> I never saw my father that much. He was in the navy ... the merchant marine and he was always at sea when I was growing up. I remember mother a lot. There were nine of us in the family. We didn't communicate that much with our mother ... she died when I was fourteen.

Tom's drinking did not diminish with his new relationship with Katie. Still an attractive man, he often drank himself into unconsciousness. United in the kinship of the bottle, he often drank with Katie's brothers from Shea Heights, then called Blackhead Road.

They were married at St. Thomas Anglican Church in St. John's, on November 23, 1968. Tom was 21 and his bride was 23. "It was a lovely evening," Katie remembered. "It was only in the chapel and we only had a few people, but at least it was a wedding."

Through his marriage to Katie and the arrival of his children, his drinking continued unabated. Katie often joined him. In spite of the love Tom and Katie had for them, the children were not being cared for properly.

The drinking often became loud and sometimes violent. Music would be blaring, people would be singing or shouting. A door would be kicked in or a drunken reveller would smash a fist through a wall. During the drinking parties, the children would usually be upstairs, often unattended. Irritated neighbours complained and then called the police.

The home on Long's Hill, when viewed through the eyes of a drunken haze, was tolerable enough. There was poverty, but problems subsided and crying children could be ignored. Young children looked through the eyes of love and the absence of any other life style with which to compare.

Before long, however, the Department of Social Services was involved, and the children were removed to temporary lodgings until Tom and Katie were better able to care for them.

The family moved to a number of other houses in the same area of the inner city, including Cabot Street, Brazil Square and McFarlane Street. Invariably the pattern would repeat itself: Pleasant Street, Anthony Avenue, Hamilton Avenue, Job Street, Forest Road, and Angel Place. "We had to move around like that because of the poor housing," Katie explained. However, there were probably other reasons as well.

Bonny King was Tammy's older sister. One of Bonny's first memories is being taken from the house by a police officer:

I was only a little girl at that time. The cop had me in his arms. I don't know how old I was but I can remember I was wrapped in a blanket and the cop was going out the door with me and I was crying. Dad was saying, 'We'll get you back. We'll get you back.'

Bonny was then handed over to a foster home. Another time, she and Tammy were taken by social workers to a home when they were about seven and five years old:

They took us in and the two of us just stood up along side the wall. Just stood there, not crying, not doing nothing.

Everyone was sitting around in the living room and the two of us just stood up by the wall. And Tammy was terrified. She cried that night. The first night we were there she cried. The woman got mad at her because she ... wet the bed. I heard her give Tammy a slap.

And I was that mad! And I just lay there in the bed. And I can remember making fists with my hands, I was that mad.

I felt like going out and choking her. That's true I did. I felt like it because she hit Tammy. That was Tammy's first night there and she was frightened. I guess the woman couldn't have understood.

But, the memory that I have of that house is good. All good, except for that first night we spent there. I can remember she bought me all kinds of new clothes and that I had a good Christmas.

Bonny was the oldest of what was by now a family of four girls, Tommy having been already placed with an adoption agency. She saw herself as the protector of her younger sisters. She remembers crying when there was nothing for them to eat.

Not all memories were bad. Bonny's fondest memories are of the hours spent in the company of her sisters.

> We used to always find ways to have fun. For one thing we were always together. We'd play together. We'd skip and play hopscotch in the summer time. We'd play hide and seek on McFarlane Street. I loved the girls. As long as we were kept together I didn't care. I felt so responsible for them.

A photo of the time shows a young looking Bonny with baby Liza in her arms. Her smile is beaming. Tammy is beside her with a more forlorn look. All appear dishevelled and unkempt.

Bonny remembers playing with Tammy on Signal Hill, St. John's most popular landmark. The girls played in the old cement bunkers left from a series of wars. These bunkers protected gun deployments, munitions and fighting men of past conflicts over the centuries. The bunkers were available recreation for the girls. They would play for hours not far from the dangerous cliffs which led to the waters of the cold North Atlantic.

Tammy was a quiet and timid young girl. She was shy and withdrawn. "Tammy kept to herself, she was quiet," Bonny remembers.

Their mother took them swimming at one of the city parks while they were living on McFarlane Street.

Another of Bonny's memories from those days relate to a Christmas at home with Tom and Katie King. There was much drinking, but not much cheer for the children. One night a knock came on their door and a man dropped off a bundle of presents from one of the local charitable organizations. The girls were in bed, but Bonny could hear her mother going through the presents and allocating them to the girls. They were already wrapped, so

Katie had to unwrap each to see if it were suitable for one of the children. Bonny never told the others what she knew about the origin of the Christmas presents, but alone she knew that they had not come from the North Pole.

Bonny longed for a closer relationship with her mother.

> I thought the world of Mom. We weren't really that close, but I wanted to be really close with her. Mom was never, never affectionate.... I can remember going up and putting my arms around her. She didn't respond. She didn't kiss me or nothing. She wasn't affectionate.

> But she was often bubbly and lively, always singing, loved to sing. She could be a bit over dramatic too.

> Dad wasn't affectionate, either. Dad was more quiet and to himself. I didn't know him, really.

McFarlane Street was the last home where Tammy lived with her father and mother. By this time the kids were being harassed by the neighbourhood children who teased and tormented them.

> There was this one fellow in particular, named Chris, and he would always pick on us. He was about twelve and I was only nine. He'd chase us on his bike and cut us off with the front wheel. He'd say, 'We called the cops on you last night. Your father is a drunk.'

> I was too scared to say anything. I'd just stand there till he stopped. He'd say it to us and he probably had a right to say it. He'd say, 'Go get ten cents and buy a bar of soap.'

> That's embarrassing.

While they were living on McFarlane Street the Social Services Dept took the children permanently from Tom and Katie. There had been an especially raucous party which climaxed when one of Katie's relatives fell or in some way was injured outside the house. The ambulance was called amid much confusion and shortly after it left with the injured party, the police arrived to take the children.

Ten year old Bonny had a little friend also named Bonny, sleeping over that night. "People next door must have phoned the cops' cause there was a racket. There was always a racket at our house. The cops seemed to be there every second day."

She looked out through the door and saw Tammy, Maggie and Liza being put in the police cruiser. She ran upstairs to alert her father and mother:

> Dad was in lying down on one of the beds, and I told him to get up. I told him, 'They're taking us! They're taking us.'

> Dad just laid there. He never opened his mouth. He just looked at me. And Mom was climbing down the ladder from the second storey to avoid the cops. I ran back down stairs and I could see Mom running down the road. She must have cut out through one of the alleys. I chased her and the cop chased me. I was shouting out to her to come back. There was a lot of ruckus and it was dark now.

> Then the cop caught hold of me and I screamed out to her not to leave us. She stopped and she came back and I said, 'You can't leave us.' She shouted that she had to run because the cops were going to arrest her.

> Mom went with us and the cops took us all and took us to the Janeway. I still don't know to this day why they took us to the

hospital. I'd say we were there for three weeks. I was about ten years old so this would be about 1980.

The hospital was OK. There was this worker in there and he was painting on the ward where we were. He used to always tell me that he was going to bring us crayons and colouring books, but he never did.

We made friends with all the nurses and the doctors and they all got to know us. We were there for quite a while. I don't know why. Probably to find a place for us.

Mom visited us once while we were in the Janeway. And Tammy cried after her and so she said she wasn't going to come back no more. And she didn't. Dad never showed up.

We loved them both and we hated to leave them. So bad as it got at home with two alcoholics we never wanted to leave. Even though we knew the lifestyle was bad and we were neglected we never wanted to leave.

This was to be Tammy's final parting from her parents. The tear-blurred vision of her mother departing the Janeway Hospital was to be the last time Tammy saw Katie. She was eight years old at the time and in a few weeks Social Services had secured foster homes for both girls on the other side of the province in Deer Lake.

For Bonny it was to be with Art and Vivien Simms. For Tammy and younger sister Maggie it was with Rita and Edward Goulding. They would stay in this home, where they were well cared for, for the next six years.

CHAPTER 4

DEER LAKE

Now as I was young and easy under the apple boughs
About the lilting house and happy as the grass was green,
The night above the dingle starry,
Time let me hail and climb
Golden in the heydays of his eyes ...

Dylan Thomas, "Fern Hill"

The three little girls stared in awe as the stewardess explained the safety regulations in English and then in French. The motors were roaring and the plane soon started down the Torbay runway at unbelievable speed. It was their first plane ride and the first time away from St. John's.

The lady in the seat beside them was a social worker, a stranger to the three small travellers. They zoomed down the runway faster than thought, faster than hope, faster than love. They hurtled away from the mother and father they loved in spite of everything.

"What pretty little girls," beamed an older lady from across the aisle.

The social worker smiled, "They're sisters."

They were on their way to their new home in Deer Lake, on the western side of the island.

Tammy, eight, sat by the aisle beside her older sister, Bonny. Tammy was feeling all the sadness of a child plucked from her home by strangers and sent to live with strangers. The busy people and the wonderful plane held no charms for her. She held back her tears and peeped around her at the smiling lady from Social Services.

Behind Tammy sat the lady from the Department of Social Services and Maggie, the youngest. Maggie looked out the window at the ground speeding by them in a blur.

Then the unbelievable happened - the plane took off from the ground and flew up into the air.

Maggie's little head was pushed back into the soft head rest behind her. But her eyes stared out the window. Her five year old body moulded itself into the back of the cushioned seat. "This is great!" she thought.

Eleven years later a bubbly sixteen year old Maggie remembered:

"I was excited. I was happy. I was on a big plane. I was in a new atmosphere. I was seeing everything. It was a lot to see at the time. I was five."

Bonny King, eleven, sat directly in front of Maggie and looked out the window too. Her mind was not in the plane. It was racing 637 kilometres ahead of the airplane to the new home at Deer Lake. She wondered what she and her sisters would find when the plane arrived there. She wondered how difficult her role as protector of the girls would be in the new home.

Experience had already taught her that foster homes were the luck of the draw. Her mind raced back to St. John's where she remembered the two foster homes they had stayed in since leaving the Janeway Hospital.

After several weeks in the Janeway Children's Hospital, the girls had been moved to a series of foster homes. Their first home had been with an older woman in a town near St. John's called Paradise. The lady's name was Mrs. Murphy. She had been kind to them and had treated them like her own.

> May be it was because she had no other kids there of her own. We were treated like 'kids'. When we wanted to, we could go out and play. When we came in, our meals were

> prepared for us. Nothing was expected of you.
> Like, you weren't expected to do everything
> for her. You weren't made to feel that you
> were intruding. We done our share of chores
> and dishes there, but she thought something
> of us. She treated us with respect.

> We weren't told that we came from
> nothing. She didn't down our parents; she
> didn't down what we came from. She
> respected us, I guess. We were treated like
> kids. We weren't talked to like ... I mean, you
> don't tell a kid they came from nothing, right?
> She was there for us. You could talk to her. It
> was different from other houses.

But their new-found joy was to be short lived. Within a few
months, Mrs. Murphy's health and age required that the girls
move. Their next home was with Cecil and Ellen Newman, also
in Paradise, where they were also treated well. "I liked them,
they treated us good," Bonny recalled. But the memories are not
as special as with Mrs. Murphy.

Bonny and her sisters were not informed as to why they were
leaving the Newman house. But, she cannot recall any feelings
of regret as they left Paradise for points unknown somewhere in
the western sky.

Their first plane ride took them to Deer Lake in about an
hour. Bonny remembered the quiet airport and the sleepy town
outside Corner Brook, then the province's second city.

> I think it was a Sunday cause on our first
> day there we drove through Main Street.
> That's where all the shops are. We were used
> to the St. John's area and I can remember
> thinking, 'My God! There's nothing here! It's
> deserted. It's so tiny and no one around.'

She was disappointed to learn that they would not be living
together in the same home. Bonny was to live with the Simms

family while Tammy and Maggie would live with Dick and Rita Goulding.

Bonny was dropped off first at the house of Vivien Simms. The Simms were a religious family of a fundamentalist sect called Pentecostal. They insisted that their foster daughter follow the same lifestyle.

> I liked going to their church, but I had to go to bed real early and they were always telling me I was going to hell. Generally they made me feel bad and guilty. I was only eleven."

Tammy and Maggie were bound for another destination. At the Goulding's house the girls saw a large back yard and heard a friendly dog bark. The house itself was a large, narrow two storey. Next door was Dick Goulding's sister and her husband.

> I remember our foster mother, Rita, picking up me and Tammy in the truck, said Maggie. I remember sitting in the living room on her lap. I was looking up at her thinking, 'You are going to be my new Mommy.' That is what I was told, too.

For the five year old Maggie King, things were never so good. She embraced her new home with an open and eager heart. In the same manner Rita and "Dick" Goulding opened their home to both girls and did all they could to make them feel welcome. They had two of their natural children still living with them: Katie, age 12 and Chris, age 10. As well, Rita had recently adopted a tiny baby, Philip.

> We were in the living room sitting down on the day that we first arrived. Dad was in the 'lazy' boy chair and there was Mom and me and Tammy and a lady, Geraldine Emberly, who was babysitting Philip. It was a happy time for me...

But Tammy looked into the living room. She still had her suitcase beside her. She looked behind her for Bonny and saw only the door. She started to cry, softly at first and then to an ever escalating crescendo of screams. She grabbed her suitcase and ran out through the door.

Near the Goulding' house is an RCMP detachment, and it was toward it that Tammy directed her flight. Screaming and racing along the road she desperately sought the only sanctuary she could find. She was chased and brought back by a surprised Goulding family.

She was calmed down and everyone tried to take the incident in stride. Her reaction was prophetic of her last desperate act, taken in anguish years later in a community whose name she had yet to hear.

Maggie's reaction was more pragmatic:

> I remember on that first day Tammy started screeching and taking her luggage and running down the road. She didn't want to be there. But I seen the big back yard we had, and there was a dog there, and I thought it was great.

> They had a beautiful big Labrador Retriever named Prince. I can remember him barking on that first day. Oh, I loved it.

> Tammy was older than me. And Bonny wasn't with us. Tammy wanted someone that she knew, and where I was so young, I was different from her, right? I was happy right from the start. A couple of weeks after we were there Mom Goulding was telling me about this little girl up the road.

> Me and Tammy were afraid to go out and meet people. But one day we went up on the back of their garden and introduced

> ourselves. Her name was Viki Caines and she
> was the same age as me. So we made a new
> friend right off the bat. We're still friends.

> I started school that September in grade
> one. Tammy was in grade three. She got to
> like it when we made new friends. We done
> excellent. At first it was hard adjusting, but
> soon it was great.

Before long Tammy was involved with her school and after-school activities. Academically she was an excellent student who maintained good grades with determined effort. She enjoyed school and the praise she received for succeeding. She took an active part in extra-curricular activities including Sea Cadets, which she thoroughly enjoyed, Church choir, and Girl Guides.

Although naturally quiet and introspective she was fun to be with in a shy kind of way. During her years in Deer Lake she grew from eight to fourteen, from grade three to grade nine. She did most of her maturing there, under the roof of Mrs. Goulding. Her personality developed in the way it had been moulded. She was happy in most things with an underlying gloom that occasionally came to the surface in a moodiness that pushed others away.

Summer weather was generally warmer and finer on the west coast of the island than in St. John's and the family enjoyed it to the full. Maggie said:

> First couple of years we had a trailer up
> in Riverside. Couple of years later we built a
> cabin up there. Me and Tammy and the other
> kids would have little cubby houses built and
> we would make little burrows in the alders
> that were cut down and play. We'd swim and
> fish and look at the beaver dam.

> Dick and Rita'd be there with their other
> friends who had foster children. Mom's good
> friend Elaine Cooper and Vivien and Art

Simms. They too, had foster kids, and we would all play around the cabins.

There was this old shack in by the cabin that we used to fill with our stuff. We called it the 'Cram-a-Lot Inn'. It was our own little hide away. We used to pretend we were like Mom and play house. We had little bunks made out of canvas and done it up like a real house.

There was an oil drum there. We used to put a big stick across it and had a see-saw. Besides that we'd be playing and riding bikes. We used to swim over to the beach and up to the cabin. We used to dive off the wharf and the bank up at the cabin. Tammy was a good swimmer.

When her father and mother seemed to have their lives back in order, the provincial Department of Social Services permitted them to contact their children. In 1984 Tammy first wrote her natural mother, Katie.

The letters Tammy wrote to her mother and father during those years provide a valuable source of information about her six years in Deer Lake. Tom and Katie King kindly offered them to be used in the research for this book.

The letters began in reply to her mother in 1984 and continued intermittently until she left Deer Lake in 1986. They were read and probably influenced by her foster mother and possibly the Social Services personnel.

Rita used to look over our shoulder when we were writing them. We'd write it and show it to her and she she'd say, 'you don't need to say that, put this in, say you're doing good,' and stuff like that. She practically wrote the letters but it was in our handwriting.

She always wanted to see what we wrote.

The letters paint a very rosy picture of her life in Deer Lake and they reflect little of any unhappiness that she was experiencing there. It does reflect, through the passage of the years and through the topics discussed, a little girl growing into a woman.

Tammy was trying to discover herself. She knew she was a foster child and that the Gouldings were not her real parents. She knew that their children were not her natural brothers and sisters. She wanted to know who she was, where she was from and who her natural family were. In this first letter she asked for pictures. This becomes a continual theme through all the letters. It is not unusual for a girl to want pictures of her separated family, but with Tammy it was a preoccupation, and part of her search for self and family. She had just turned twelve years old on November 9. This is the first letter in its entirety with Tammy's grammar and punctuation intact.

December 17, 1984

Dear Mom:

I have not been writing you since now because I wasn't allowed to. I would like to know how you're doing. Recently I got my report card back. These are my marks: Math A+ 92 and I got an A, 81 English. Religion I got 100%. French - A Geography - A, History B. Home Economics - 100%.

Mom - I would like to have some pictures of me when I was a baby if you got any and could you please tell me who my grandparents are on your side of the family and on dad's side.

If you got a tape recorder Maggie and I will make a tape and tell you what we got for Christmas.

Where was I born in what hospital? Do you know where Liza our baby sister is? or our brothers?

I'm now in grade 7, 12 years old. My foster parents are very special to me. I just recently started babysitting. I would like to have a picture of you. I love you. My foster parents told me this is my home as long as I want it to be.

XOXO XOXO
XOXO
Love Tammy.
XOXO

PS I don't have my school pictures back for this year so I will send you one of last years and one of the pictures when I was confirmed.

The last sentence before her signature is a comforting thought, however it was unfortunately not reflected in the circumstances of her leaving the home two years later.

There may have been letters lost in the interim, and delays sending the letters through the Department of Social Services, but the next letter is dated six months later. No return address was given on the top of these early letters, probably to protect the children from unwanted contact by the real parents. This letter too is printed in its entirety.

June 27, 1985

Dear Mom:

How are you doing? Well I'm fine.

Thanks for the picture of yourself but I can't pick you out. Thanks for the watch but it was broken.(No need to buy me things anyway.)

I passed with a diploma and with good marks in my report card.

Mom, I do remember Tina and Peter. Could you please send me a picture of Betty.

That negative you wanted is lost. That picture was taken a couple years ago and it was only me who was confirmed. Maggie was not old enough.

Well, This week passed was swimming and fishing up to our cabin. I loves it. I Love you and I miss you very much! Gotta go now write soon! I will!

Love Tammy
XOXOXO
Love
XOXOXO
Sorry
So
Short

Tammy's parents had now been separated for some time. In 1985 her father, too, had approached the Department of Social Services, Child Welfare Division, with a view to contacting his children. Soon Tammy would be writing him as well.

August 6, 1985

Dear Mom:

How are you? I'm fine. I'm glad to hear from you to. I saw the social worker today, she wanted to speak to us about our father. What she told us was Dad has given up drinking for the passed year now and he told the social worker he wanted to have contact with us by writing letters. Dad works at odd jobs around. The social worker said he is trying to work hard and I am very glad to hear that ...

I hope you get a job.

I did enjoy my summer holidays. I am going up to our cabin tomorrow. I have many good friends that go up to the cabin ...

Mom I have my ears pierced but I'll keep the earrings as souvenirs. Nobody wears those earrings any more.

Mom is Marina living up there? I don't know what any of my relatives look like. But I'd like to know what they look like, that's why I'd like pictures of them. I'd get a bigger album and it will be my family.

I remember Marina. Have she got a boyfriend or is she married. Thanks for trying to get a picture of yourself. I wanna know what you look like ...

I don't remember Joan/ Bob or Irene King. Bonita, I don't know her at all. How old is Marina, Betty and Joan?...

Tammy had been separated from her real family since 1980 and she often searched her memories for faces of her antecedents. She questioned her sisters about the past, and picked through their memories. Photographs held time still and allowed her to know an aspect of herself that she could not know in Deer Lake.

The next letter to her mother was less than a page long.

November 29, 1985

Dear Mom:

How are you. I'm fine. Bonny is now living at our foster mother's aunt and uncle's place. They're very nice people. So we see Bonny often. Mom, if you want to get me a Christmas gift I'd like a picture of you that I can pick out and an album from you. I'm sending a picture of me inside. It was taken Nov 4, 1985, My school picture this year. I'm in the sea cadets now and I love it. It's the best thing I ever got in.

Mom, I'm not interested in any gifts. I just want to see what you and dad looks like that's what I would like: a picture I like to see what you looks like after 6 years. I don't have a clue what you look like now.

I know that when two people cannot get along they are better off separated so you don't need to explain that story and what happened ...

I miss you!

Love Tammy
XOXO

In the next letter, dated March 5, 1985, Tammy asked:

Thanks for the information on my life.... Where do Vinnicombe and Frank Tucker live (my grandparents). And where do the King's (my grandparents on Dad's side of the family live now). Mom where is our father living? Did you give up drinking? Are you living with your boyfriend?

In the same letter, Tammy confides to her mother, "We were taking sex education and in January the 8th I started my first period. I had 2 periods I'm growing into an adult now."

By November Tom King had established written contact with his daughters through the Department of Social Services. On November 29, 1985 Tammy wrote her first letter to her dad:

"I've been waiting six years to see what you look like and now I have the chance." Soon she was asking him for information about her real family:

> Do I have any relatives in St. John's?
> Mom (real one) sent me some pictures of
> herself and Tina - Peter's daughter and June
> and many more pictures of our cousins.

Sometimes Tammy saw herself as a conduit of communications between her real parents. She wrote her father March 15, 1986, "Our mother called Thursday night she said for me to say Hi to you for her."

Immediate hopes of a renewed relationship with her mother were crushed soon after that letter. She wrote her father on April 2, 1986:

> Our mother called us Saturday night.
> She was really rude. She had told us on the
> letters that she was not drinking and when she
> phoned, she was drunk.

Tammy would not write her mother again for more than two years, just before she died. Letters to 'Dear Dad' continued with great affection leading up to his visiting his three daughters in the summer of 1986.

In April 26, 1986 she wrote him:

> How's Tina & Audrey, Peter and Peter.
> I'm gonna write them soon. She (Audrey)
> wrote me & Maggie not too long ago. She sent
> some pictures of Her & Peter at their cabin.

> One of the whole family with your sister
> Katie. One of Tommy and her is gorgeous. On
> the picture he is about 4 or 5. And she sent a
> picture of me & Peter (younger Peter) I am
> about 5 or 6 in the picture.

She looked forward with great expectation to seeing her father after so many years. For Tammy, all the questions would then be answered. All the yearning for family and self knowledge would be satisfied. All the pictures would finally come to life in the person of her longed for father.

In August of 1986, Tom King drove out to Deer Lake with his brother Peter, Peter's wife Audrey, and their two children.

The visit to Deer Lake began badly. Audrey's brother, travelling with them in his own car, suffered a seizure at the campground near Gander. Half way across the island they found themselves on a hospital ward, phoning Rita Goulding to explain their delay. When they were confident of his recovery, they left the brother in Gander and proceeded west. They covered the same general route travelled by the three little girls and the social worker, six summers before, in the plane.

Then car problems plagued and further delayed them. Finally, they arrived in Deer Lake. They went on a few miles to Gros Morne National Park and pitched their tents. It was now late in the day and they were tired, so they decided to wait until the next day to go to Deer Lake and the foster home.

Next day, the family was quiet in the car as Peter looked for the Goulding's house. Audrey was concerned about the reception they would be given by the foster parents, especially after they had been forced to change the arrangements in mid trip.

"What do these people think of us?" she kept thinking. The foster parents knew that the children had been removed from the King home and they knew about the drinking and marital strife.

As well, Audrey was concerned how the girls would react to their father and natural family. Would resentment or anger surface at the first meeting since that terrible night on McFarlane Street? Would there be embarrassing questions or, worse still, unspeaking, questioning eyes, or muttered sarcasm?

When they finally arrived at the Goulding house, the tired travellers were well received by Rita Goulding in spite of their late arrival.

They were ecstatically received by the two sisters who flocked out on the driveway to meet them. There was some awkwardness as the introductions were made, but when Tammy put her arms around her cousins, uncle, aunt and her father, the warmth of the feelings were real on both sides.

Rita Goulding looked on as her foster children hugged their natural father, surrounded by exuberant relatives. She was a reserved woman, not given to demonstrations of affection. She knew those things as transitory. Instead she offered steady care and concern that did not flash brightly one day and disappear the next.

She knew that the two girls were cared for and fed better under her roof than they had ever been by Tom and Katie King. But there was something jarring about the almost palpable love that surrounded the group of huddling celebrants who hugged and kissed each other in her yard. The scene was exciting and inviting but she could not join.

The dog, Prince, barked from behind the house where he was tied. Perhaps he wanted to join the joyous activity. She looked up and in spite of the joy in the yard a note of sadness came into her heart. It was like the darkness descending across the land. Rita knew that things would never be the same again.

The travellers were invited in for a cup of tea and everyone was as pleasant as possible under the circumstances. Then the three sisters bundled into Peter's car and they drove back to their camp site at Gros Morne Park. It was quite a bundle as the three adults and five teenagers crammed into the Dodge Omni hatchback. Tammy, Maggie and cousin Tina jumped over the back seat into the trunk amid gleeful laughter.

The happy scene in that crowded car was of another world. Tom King looked at his beautiful daughters bundled in the car's interior. The girls bubbled away, mostly to each other. Tammy stole careful glances at her father. A tired Peter sped the little Omni towards Gros Mourne Park.

At the Deer Lake junction they turned north and drove up the

Great Northern Peninsula of Newfoundland. Soon they were in the looming hills and deep valleys of Gros Morne.

The very name, Gros Morne, suggests a great tragedy, a heavy foreboding. This park is a massive backdrop for any occasion. The cliffs of billion year old rock, 20 times as old as the Rockies, loom towards the eternal sky. Glacial fiords 130 meters deep are filled with clear fresh water. In the park is the "Tablelands", a huge slab of the earth's inner mantle shoved violently upwards to the surface of an ancient ocean. This occurred 450 million years ago when Europe and North America collided in a massive continental drift. Every rock can tell an ancient story of creation, plate tectonics, and continental movement.

There are volcanic sea stacks and caves along Gros Morne's 72 kilometres of coast line. Also along the shore line grow the tuckamores - pygmy evergreens, spruce and fir - whose growth was stunted by the cold wind and salt spray from the Atlantic. They are kin to the krumholz of the Alps.

Like lost souls, families of them cling to one another and form impenetrable phalanxes of green boughs and needles. They survive on this bleak coast only because they huddle together, supporting and protecting one another from the wind and cold. They grow together in tangled, knotted masses of life, hemmed in by a sea of cold ancient rock on one side, and the older, colder salt sea on the other.

Human settlement at Gros Morne has been recent - a mere 4500 years. Maritime Archaic and Beothuk Indians were two of the better known peoples who lived in Gros Morne before the Europeans arrived. Each tribe and people had come, celebrated their brief lives, and disappeared from the park, and sometimes from the planet. The eternal rocks looked down on all.

These same rocks looked down upon the revels of the King family in August of 1986.

Away from the foster parents, the family felt less awkward, and the kids lightened the tension with their amiable chatter. The young people established an immediate rapport with each other that the adults found difficult to duplicate.

A combination of factors and a mix of personal chemistries

were at work as they walked in the park that day. No one wanted to eat supper or to see the day end. They walked and talked more quietly now; much was said and much more was left unsaid. The five teenagers mulled together and walked or sat as a group, chatting.

Audrey King felt a difficulty in reaching the girls at a meaningful level on so sudden and short a meeting. They were obviously happy to see their father. They hugged and beamed and talked eagerly to him. But the gulf of six years and the memories of the painful past still separated them like a glacial gorge between its two shores.

Too soon they had to return the girls to their foster homes. The happily-bundled Omni found its way to the Goulding and Simms foster homes. Fond "til tomorrows" were exchanged and a beautiful day in the lives of them all came to a sweet end at their campsite in Gross Morne.

The next day was warm and sunny. In the morning the Dodge Omni was once again stuffed with eight happy Kings as they headed for nearby Memorial Park. They picked up chicken at a local take out and went to the park to eat. There is a beautiful sandy beach in the park where the kids and Audrey went swimming. Tom and Peter watched from the shore.

The two men chatted between themselves and may even have thought about the last time they were in Deer Lake together in 1965, more than twenty years before. They had been about the same age of their frolicking kids in the water. The brothers had been on the "Newfie Bullet", on their way to the promised land of Toronto, without money to buy a meal when they had arrived.

They still wore the scars of those days as they watched the revellers in the pure, blue water. The water of Deer Lake splashed and gleamed where the sun struck it; silver streaks amid the deepest, brightest blue; bluer than a child's eyes.

On August 11, Tammy wrote her dad about that visit:

> I am so happy to have seen you after all
> this time. I love you very, very, very much and
> I always will. It seemed as though I had a lot
> to tell you and ask you but I really didn't

know how. I wanted to sit here and write you tonight because you're very special and you are always on my mind and in my heart.... You looked very handsome and everyone said we have your big brown eyes and long eyelashes, and we look just like you.

So I'll write again as soon as possible. And you know, no matter what everything turns out like, I'll always love you very much. I miss you already.

Love,
Tammy XOXOXOXOXOXOXOXOX
XOXOXOXOXOXOXOXOXOX"

The second last sentence reads ominously prophetic. The turning wheels of the gods were about to take another turn for Tammy and her two sisters.

Trouble was already brewing in Deer Lake. The end of the summer of 1986 was bringing a change of weather that filled the air. The late-summer rain fell in thick sheets across the lake. Cool winds off the Atlantic kicked at the large, black hammerhead clouds high up over the troubled waters of the lake.

Beothuk Indians had once looked up at these clouds from their campgrounds in the same spot where Tammy and her family had frolicked. The lake was special to the Indians because of the migrating caribou herds that crossed it and on which the Beothuk depended for survival.

Caribou and Beothuk romped there no more. Both had long since been exterminated by the white culture of gentleman adventurers. The caribou were now relegated to protected areas of the province, while the Indians were wiped forever from the face of the earth.

In the sudden, late August coolness, the sandy beach lay empty and the face of the sun was hidden in the cloaks of black clouds. An ill wind whipped the rain into cold sheets and whipped them against the soft sand. Soon the steady showers began, signalling an imminent end to the warm weather and the coming of September and autumn.

Perhaps Tammy was aware of the trouble that was soon to end her six year stay in Deer Lake. As well, it was to end her childhood and her innocence.

Her last two letters to her father, Tom King, contain none of the laudatory references to her happy foster home. There was trouble.

Perhaps the renewed relationship with her real family had weakened the bonds between Tammy and her foster family. In spite of the rosy optimism pervasive in Tammy's letters, there had always been some friction in the Goulding foster home.

There was the normal friction between the natural children and the two girls. Sometimes the sisters were abruptly reminded by the Goulding children of their temporary status in the home. Name-calling and verbal sparring is a normal part of many healthy sibling relationships.

There was the normal clash between Tammy and her younger sister Maggie, which escalated toward the end of their stay in Deer Lake. For example, Tammy would be allowed to attend teen dances and Maggie would not. This would cause dissent in the home as Rita tried to raise her own children and her two growing foster children. With the added attention needed by her adopted son, who was younger than them all, Rita was finding it more and more a strain to do justice to her extended family.

There were some later references to personal problems Tammy was having at the time and meetings in the house with the social worker and Rita. Maggie recalled:

> I don't know why we left Deer Lake. I'm still confused about that. Some problems with Tammy and Rita. Later Rita told me Tammy was supposed to get some help for it in St. John's.

> In another way Rita was good to us. She fed us well and she clothed us well. We didn't have to worry about other kids making fun of us at school. I have mixed feelings about the home.

As well there was the security of a stable home. In spite of internal squabbles the girls had a deep emotional bond to Rita Goulding and their home with her.

Their last night in Deer Lake was a sad one. Rita came in the girls' room to help with their packing. Maggie looked at her half-packed suitcase and for the first time, the twelve year old realized that she was really leaving what had been her home since she was five. Tears filled her eyes and she started to sob. Soon she was gasping and bawling her heart out. "Why are we leaving?" she asked through her tears.

Tammy could see that Rita, their mother for the last seven years, was crying too.

"It's better this way for everyone."

Behind them Tammy sat down and cried on her own bed.

The next morning they all had breakfast together. The three of them sat at the kitchen table and Rita was upbeat. "Be sure and phone me as soon as you get in Deep Harbour."

Tammy nodded.

"Write me and tell me how you are getting on in your new home."

"OK, Mom, we'll write."

"And you'll be near your real parents and your relatives in Mount Pearl."

But when they were going out through the door her feelings for the girls broke through and once again Rita cried.

Tammy looked again at the big yard and heard Prince bark a farewell salute. Perhaps the retriever knew that Tammy would never come back; that she would not be retrieved alive from a sea of cold, dark water far away.

Her own heart was filled with trouble that she did not express nor even understand. As usual she hid her feelings well and smiled as the social worker wished her a good morning.

His name was Don Evans and he was bringing the girls to their new foster home in Deep Harbour. He had taken his wife and infant child along as well.

I wanted to go back home; we both did.
I mean, I cried most of the way there in
silence to myself and I know Tammy did too.
We didn't want to be leaving and sent to a

place we didn't know, with strange people,
right. It was confusion in our heads.

The seven hour drive ended around 2:30 pm in Deep
Harbour. Evans' car approached the Weller home on the old
highway.

Her life in Deer Lake was over and that time of her life
closed off behind her like the waters closed in on the wake of a
motor boat. The wheels of the gods continued to grind without
giving reasons. She found herself at the home of strange, new
foster parents.

Her older sister, Bonny was far behind in Deer Lake with
Art and Vivien Simms. At least her sister Maggie was with her.
In ten days she would celebrate her fourteenth birthday.

CHAPTER 5

Dawn Williams

I punish the children for the sins of the fathers to
the third and fourth generations ...

Deuteronomy 5:9

The story of sexual abuse in the Weller family began long
before Tammy and Maggie arrived in 1986. Like many dark
family secrets, it was not restricted to one generation nor restricted
to one house. This book traces the abuse back only to 1974 with
the arrival of a pretty 9 year old girl named Dawn Williams.

Tammy and Maggie were not the first girls to arrive at a
Weller foster home in Deep Harbour. Albert Weller's brother
Levi lived next door. In 1973 Levi, 36, and his wife, Mary, 34,
had four children of their own, three boys and a girl. They
wanted a playmate for their youngest child, a daughter, age ten.
Levi was a heavy equipment operator who owned his own home,
a clean, three bedroom bungalow.

The social worker who interviewed the prospective foster
parents wrote enthusiastically:

> Mr. Weller stands six feet tall and
> weighs approximately 190 lbs. He has greying
> black hair, grey eyes and medium
> complexion. A friendly man he converses
> easily and intelligently - possesses a good

> sense of humour and appears to be respected
> and well liked by members of the community.
> Mr. Weller is active in church and school
> activities but spends most of his leisure time
> with his family - whether it be outings or
> making improvements to his home.

These comments reflected the views of many who knew and liked the Weller family. A letter of reference from the parish priest has somewhat less adulation as it comments: "They appear to be doing well at raising their own children."

On May 25, 1973 Levi and his wife were granted a licence to operate a foster home. They had specifically requested a nine year old female child. On January 10, 1974 six year old Dawn Williams became the second foster child to live there.

Like Tammy, Dawn had come from an unhappy background. When she was born her mother, Theresa, had no husband and lived in fear of an alcoholic father. Theresa was the second oldest of thirteen children. Her family life could be described as unhappy, partly because of her father's frequent drinking and violence.

Dawn's mother, Theresa, 19, had been unsuccessful in her grade ten exams and subsequently quit school. She had worked variously as a waitress, factory worker and domestic. Theresa liked to work as it took her out of the house where there was so much tension and unhappiness. She also liked to forget her problems through an active social life.

In May, 1967, three months before Dawn was born, Theresa visited her welfare officer who wrote:

> Miss Williams is of slight build and is
> five foot four inches tall. She usually weighs
> about 108 pounds. She has green eyes and a
> light complexion. Her hair, which is blond,
> has been bleached to a yellowy-blond. She
> could be described as attractive but her bright
> yellow hair rather cheapens her general
> appearance. She is otherwise well groomed
> and neat.

> She is a self confident, assured girl who
> was straight-forward and well-spoken during
> my dealings with her. She seemed to be of
> average intelligence. She didn't seem to be
> concerned about her situation as far as the
> child was concerned but is afraid that her
> father will discover her condition.

Theresa refused to name Dawn's father but described him a six foot mechanic, 19 years of age. He had blue eyes, dark red hair. She said that she was no longer dating the man and did not want to marry him. The reasons she gave the welfare officer were that he was a heavy drinker and of a different religious faith, Roman Catholic.

Theresa indicated that she wanted what was best for her unborn baby and she felt that was to place the child for adoption.

On July 5, 1967 Dawn was born at St. Clare's Hospital in St. John's. She was baptised a Catholic and Theresa indicated the child's religion as Catholic when she signed "Consent to Adoption" papers a week later.

Dawn came under the care and control of the Child Welfare Division of the Newfoundland Department of Social Services on July 12, 1967. The director of Child Welfare for the province of Newfoundland was authorized by documents Theresa signed to:

> ... take the said child into his care and
> custody and to do all things as he may
> consider advisable or necessary in respect to
> the health and well-being of the said child ...

The Director became Dawn's legal guardian. But this standard agreement, signed by a troubled, single mother, curiously contained a clause which pointed out that the director did not "incur any responsibility or liability" in the execution of these responsibilities. In other words he had the control of Dawn's life without any responsibility if it went wrong.

On July 21st, two weeks after her birth, Dawn was placed in a foster home in Mount Pearl to await adoption.

Her Child Progress Report for October 25th of the same year relates that, "she is developing normally. She has blue eyes, brown hair and a fair complexion."

Then the welfare officer prophetically adds, "She seldom smiles and has a 'far away' look on her face."

Was the infant's 'far away look' in the direction of her mother's home? Or was she looking much farther away than that? Perhaps even into the future to the home of Levi Weller and the unhappiness that would befall her there. If so, it were reason enough not to smile.

A later report says, "...nice looking child with blue eyes." Dawn's mother, Theresa was now visiting weekly. In March of the next year, Theresa indicated to the Welfare Department that she and her new boyfriend were planning to get married and were only waiting for him to secure work. Dawn's adoption was put on hold pending developments in her mother's life.

In September 1968 a social worker reported that Dawn was:

> ... a very pretty child with curly, blond hair and blue eyes. She seems happy and contented. She shows no fear of strangers.

In August, 1968 Theresa married the new boyfriend, Dean Smith, and requested that the Department of Welfare return her child. Her own mother was separated from her drunken husband and was ready to help care for the child when Theresa was working. Things seemed to be looking up for everyone.

On November 1st, 1968, Theresa had the Family Court judge rescind her "Consent to Adoption"; this secured the return of her child. Dawn could not be returned immediately, however, for she was in hospital with a case of pneumonia.

The family experiment of Dawn, her mother and step-father did not work. The 29-year-old Dean was consumed with jealousy of his wife's past relationship. As he looked at Dawn he saw a constant reminder of that relationship and his feeling cooled toward the child.

Dean Smith had completed high school and one year at university. He had tried numerous occupations before becoming a supervisor with the federal government. It was a good job, but previous debts kept the family from financial security.

Theresa and Dean Smith had a son born to them in May, 1970. Dean doted on his son, but it only increased his resentment against Dawn. His memory of the past was constantly jogged by the little, blond reminder toddling about his floor.

As she got older Dawn came to realize that Dean did not care for her. She tried to win his affection in the simple ways of a three year old. He would be sitting on a couch and she would climb up beside him. He would ignore her or turn away to read a newspaper or watch TV.

But he did not ignore her if she misbehaved. Slight infractions and imagined infractions were dealt with severely. Dawn was often locked in her room with the lights out. Physical punishment was not uncommon.

There was little or no affection shown by either parent to the child. Dawn was rarely ever kissed or held or offered the normal emotional food children need.

Dean often turned to alcohol to soothe his inner demons of jealousy and inadequacy. This sometimes resulted in aggression and violence directed at Theresa and Dawn. At other times Dean would withdraw into his own mind to avoid unpleasant memories or discussions.

One night in 1972 Theresa returned home to find Dean attempting to rape her thirteen year old sister. The girl had been visiting the house at the time. She reported it to the police but charges that followed were dropped and the incident was covered up by the family.

These and other troubles beset them. Theresa became convinced that there could be no hope for happiness in their home as long as Dawn remained. She could see some hope for a future for Dean, herself and their new son. The tension that Dawn triggered in Dean was making life unbearable for all of them.

On January 3, 1974 Theresa was back to the Department of Welfare signing new "Consent to Adoption" papers. A week later Dawn was brought by the social worker to the Levi Weller household.

Dean Smith did not ask his wife what had happened to Dawn; he never spoke her name again.

Dawn's new life was in Deep Harbour. Life in a new home was exciting for a six year old. Dawn remembers that first day at the Weller home. She was accompanied from St. John's by the welfare officer. She clutched a bag of toys which she gleefully dumped out on the day bed in the kitchen. She had no idea who these friendly new people were and what she was doing there, but they seemed nice to her.

She was also unclear why she would not be living with her real mother although she did not miss her step-father. In fact the child was filled with a fear of Dean. His jealousy and bitterness had often translated itself into meanness and retribution against her.

Welfare office Joan Yeates wrote of Dawn:

> After the birth of Dean and Theresa's son, all attention focused on him and it was at this time that Theresa found herself completely turning away from Dawn and it got to the point where she couldn't stand her near and couldn't bear to hold her or kiss her.

> She said that she gave up physically punishing her in fear that she wouldn't be able to control herself and would badly hurt her. Dawn's terrified behaviour after she came into care indicates that she was unnecessarily punished by someone.

The Wellers noted that Dawn was pleasant yet somewhat wild and difficult to control at times. She was already a very troubled child. Dawn was possessed by a deep inner fear. The security of a mother and father that most children can rely on had been denied to her. Even siblings to share her troubles had been denied. At six she was alone among strangers with much psychological damage already done.

Fear filled Dawn's first days and weeks at the Weller home.

She seemed to expect harsh physical punishment for even slight misdeeds. She was afraid to go to sleep with the lights off. She told Mrs. Weller that she had often been locked in her room in the dark.

The kindness extended to her by the Wellers seemed to change her during the first few months there. They had expected a child three years older as a playmate for their daughter, Louise. However, in spite of this, they seemed to accept Dawn without reservation.

Before long everyone could notice a change in the child. She seemed to get over her fears and settle in to life in Deep Harbour. The excessive demand for attention often observed in foster children upon arrival soon abated. She played happily on the large expanse of open ground that surrounded the Weller brothers' houses. There were woods and ponds near by. She swam and fished in summer; she rode her bike and played with the other children; she skidooed and skated in winter.

Sometimes she played with the children from the houses next door. They were also Wellers, cousins of her foster family. Albert, Pat, and Frank were Levi's younger brothers. Allan was Levi's father.

By her seventh birthday on July 5, 1974, Dawn was as happy a little girl as you would expect to find. She was very pretty in an active tom-boy way. She had bright blue eyes and average height and weight.

Staff at the Janeway Hospital's Communication Development Clinic saw Dawn and Mrs. Weller that month. Mrs. Weller described Dawn's fear of being returned to her mother's home. The child now called Levi and Mary "Mom and Dad".

She appeared to be thriving in her new location. She was fond of the Weller family and seemed to have a special fondness for her foster father, Levi. The observant worker also noted that the child was very quiet and did not respond to questions of a personal or emotional nature. Strangely, the worker noted that although the girl could write and draw for her, she could not or would not produce a figure of a man.

The long term intention of the authorities was to have Dawn adopted, in compliance with her mother's wish. Her stay at the

Wellers' was to be temporary, however beneficial. The Wellers indicated that they were not in a financial position to adopt the child since they needed the monthly welfare payments for her continued maintenance.

In fact Dawn was not the first apparent success story of the Wellers. Just before her arrival the family had taken an emergency case. A mistreated and mal-nourished girl had stayed there and been restored to good health and subsequently returned to her parents by the Welfare Department.

The plan for Dawn, however, was that adoption would be preferable to extended foster care. This feeling is well represented by Dr. Doherty at the Janeway Hospital on February 18, 1975:

> In July 1974 I felt very strongly that adoption was contrary to this child's best interest. However, Dawn has changed dramatically. Since the Wellers are not in a financial position to adopt her, possible adoptive parents should be sought.

> Mrs. Weller expressed doubts about the successful conclusion of any venture designed to remove her from their household. However, long term planning for her certainly involves a sincere effort to have her adopted. If all else fails then certainly permanent Foster placement should be in this home.

A month later, in March of 1975 Dawn's social worker made her regular Child Progress report. In it she noted: "Dawn really loves this couple and looks upon them as her family. She is very attached to Mr. Weller."

Dawn was progressing well in grade two at the local school in Deep Harbour. She had many friends in the community especially around her home. She was not happy with the doctor's recommendation that she leave the Wellers for adoption, and she communicated this to the social worker. The worker's final comment was, "Go very slowly with the adoption plans."

However, in spite of eight-year-old Dawn's feelings on the matter, Mrs. Weller's cautions, and the welfare worker's recommendation, the adoption process was initiated. Dawn was taken to Corner Brook where she was placed in the home of a single mother, Julia Walsh. Julia had a daughter of her own and perhaps Dawn was intended to be a playmate for the other little girl.

Dawn had pleasant memories of her stay in Corner Brook and kind things to say about Julia Walsh. In spite of good intentions, however, there were problems from the beginning. Julia remarked to the social worker that Dawn was rather rough and tumble, a bit of a tom-boy, quite unlike her own daughter.

In February of 1976 Julia talked with the social worker. She admitted that in spite of what appeared to be a successful placement, she had so far been unable to feel any closeness with the child. The maternal warmth that she felt for her own child was absent when it came to Dawn. The social worker replied that it usually takes time for a close relationship to develop with a child of Dawn's age and Julia should give it time.

Julia also complained that Dawn was such an outgoing child and constantly involved in games and physical activities. Julia had rheumatoid arthritis which made it difficult for her to keep up with a very kinetic Dawn. Finally Julia requested that the probationary period in which she would have to make her final decision to adopt Dawn be extended beyond the usual six months.

Dawn's memories of this period are positive and happy ones, but Dawn was not as happy an eight year old as her recollections may suggest. There was not a good relationship between the two children in the house. There were discipline problems with Dawn that Julia didn't always know how to handle. Julia was put off by Dawn's emotional independence and observed that Dawn would be just as happy to be separated from her. As well, Julia was still unable to establish any feelings of closeness with the child.

Dawn missed the presence of a male figure in the Walsh house. She would spend a lot of time with a family nearby where there were men.

On June 17, 1976 the Program Consultant responsible for her

case reviewed the situation at Dawn's Corner Brook home and recommended that she be returned to a foster home, preferably the Weller home in Deep Harbour, if they were willing to take her.

They were. Dawn finished out the school year in Corner Brook and on July 8, 1976, three days after her ninth birthday, she was returned to the Levi Weller home.

A social worker reporting on the home two weeks later wrote that, "It appears to be a very happy home with an abundance of love and understanding." The worker continues:

> I feel that it was quite fortunate for Dawn that she could return to the Weller family. They are a warm affectionate family and Mr. and Mrs. Weller are mature sensible adults. I feel Dawn will do well here and recommend continued use of this home as a foster family.

Welfare officer, Bonita Rush, wrote Dawn's Child Progress Report in April, 1977. She reported glowingly of the foster home, noting as well the presence of two teenage sons and a thirteen year old daughter living at home. The report ended:

> Dawn should remain in this foster home where she is perfectly happy and content. She has developed strong emotional ties with her foster parents and feels as though she belongs in this family. Mr. Weller is the only father figure she has ever known and she is very attached to him.

Other glowing reports follow through the next five years: November 1977; June 5, 1978; April 11, 1979; June 1980; and July 1981.

But all was not well in the Levi Weller household. Social workers like Bonita Rush, overworked with their heavy caseloads, had few powers to discern the inner chemistry of a foster home. To the workers the emotional climate inside those homes was an uncharted country whose horizon stopped as the back door closed behind them.

Shortly after Dawn, aged nine, returned to Deep Harbour in 1976, Levi Weller began touching her body for sexual purposes. The circumstances appeared innocent on the surface. His wife, Mary, was working the four to twelve shift in a nearby restaurant. The social workers were impressed that the husband would step in to assume the responsibility for the children during those hours. On other nights Mary and often Louise would attend bingo, a local parish fund raiser.

The two older boys were on the mainland for most of the next ten years. During these nights Levi would often be alone with Dawn. The lights would be out in the living room. The television would be the only light in the room. The drapes would be closed.

Dawn's first sexual experience with Levi Weller was one night when the two of them were alone in the house. They were watching television with him lying on the sofa and her sitting in the armchair. Levi got up and closed the drapes. He then went to his bedroom and returned with a blanket. He lay back down on the sofa and said, "Dawn, come over and lie down with Daddy."

She left her chair and the two of them cuddled on the sofa. This relationship with her foster father was the closest, most secure one the nine year old had ever known. It felt as if she were finally receiving the love withheld by an absent father and a violently abusive step-father. Under the warm blanket, the nine year old girl felt surrounded by a sea of love and security by her foster father.

But that soon changed as his hand slipped under her clothes. Dawn turned on her back as Levi slid his hand down under her pants and undies. He ran his hand all over her body, centring on her vaginal area.

At first this surprised the child. She obviously lacked experience or instruction in the area of human sexuality, and was quite at a loss to understand his intent. But it soon became apparent as his ardour increased along with the intensity of his touching.

This continued for ten or fifteen minutes. He inserted his

finger into her vagina. This incident came to an end when she, frightened and confused, pushed his hand away and jumped up from the chesterfield. She ran into the bedroom she shared with his daughter, Louise and cried.

The exchange was almost entirely non-verbal. Soon there were repetitions of this event. The next night she was alone with Levi, Dawn was nervous. She still loved him although she did not understand what the touching was all about. This was still the happiest home she had known and she could not think about doing anything to lose it.

"Come over and lie down with Daddy, Dawn." His voice was soft but insistent. They were alone, and she came over. She slid onto the couch with him and soon the touching began.

When Dawn was shaken by her first orgasm at age nine the experience was beyond her comprehension. She was unprepared intellectually or emotionally. She was frightened by the confused emotions she was feeling and could not sort out. There was the sexual pleasure, so incomprehensible to a nine year old, but powerful nontheless. There were other feelings of doubt and embarrassment.

Once or twice a week Levi and Dawn had their encounters on the living room couch: drapes closed, lights out, blanket, no one else home. Levi would take her hand and put it down inside his pants. Soon, her hand would bring him to orgasm. Usually there was mutual orgasm. Then, without a word he would quickly get up and go into the bathroom to clean up.

Sometimes there was a brief struggle. Once Dawn recalls crawling under the chesterfield and Levi pulling her out by the legs, firmly but not violently. His advances were not rough, violent or accompanied by verbal threats. Also there was no game playing that involved the child in sexual encounters as has been reported in other cases of this kind.

Once someone came home and interrupted them. Levi jumped up from the chesterfield and rushed into the bathroom. Left on the chesterfield, Dawn recalls the feeling of fear when she saw how terrified Levi was. The fear of being caught was real for him and it prompted her to think that there was something very bad in what they were doing. She jumped up and ran to her room, more confused than ever. In her room she cried alone and shook uncontrollably.

This sexual activity with Levi Weller continued until Dawn was fourteen. During that time she told two other people.

Billy Weller was Levi's youngest son. He was fifteen in 1976 when Dawn was nine. It was Billy, not Louise, in whom Dawn first confided about the sexual activities with their father. In the confused words of a nine-year-old, she told Billy that his father had touched her and how they had both orgasmed.

> Billy thought it was a big joke, he just laughed. He was amazed and said he couldn't believe it. He found it really funny.

Shortly after that Billy took the nine year old into his bedroom and asked her to take off her clothes. She refused at first, but soon he was having sex with her too.

If there was no one at home he would take her into his bedroom and take off her clothes.

> Once he brought me into the bedroom and threw me on the bed and started taking off all my clothes and tried to have sexual intercourse ... he got on top of me and tried to put his penis in my vagina. I started to scream ... he put it in so far and it started to hurt me and I told him to stop.

The sexual intercourse with Billy began when Dawn was about twelve. Sometimes it took place outdoors behind the house. She remembers it as unfeeling and taking advantage of her. She felt that the older boy was enjoying the control over her as much as the sex.

Often Billy and she would be home with Levi watching television. Levi would fall asleep and Billy would indicate to her that he wanted her to go out doors and wait for him. She would go out behind the house and wait. Soon he would follow her and they would have sex.

"Why did you go?" I once asked Dawn.

"I thought I had to."

"Couldn't you tell someone?"

"I told Billy and look what that got me."

"Didn't you know it was wrong?"

"How was I supposed to know? I mean his father was doing it to me."

Levi's brother, Albert, lived next door and would often visit. These visits became a trial for Dawn, especially if she were alone in the house at the time. On many occasions, Albert would grab at her, sometimes in a playful way but later in a more sexual manner. He would touch her by grabbing her breasts outside her clothes. He would grab her and push his hand inside her pants and touch her.

Sometimes he would see her from his yard. "Who's home, Dawn?" If nobody else was, he would come over. "Want to go in to my cabin with me, Dawn? I can pick up a bottle and we can have some fun."

The cabin was on an island in Deep Harbour Pond. Sometimes the families went there but Dawn never did go alone with Albert. But Levi's brother Albert would soon have his own foster daughter to take to the cabin in Deep Harbour Pond. Her name was Tammy King.

The old man of this clan was Allan Weller, father of Albert, Frank, Pat and Levi, and a daughter. Dawn had to be vigilant not to allow herself to be caught alone with the old man either. He would pull her onto his knee and try to touch her inside her clothes. She saw him do this with other children as well.

Several of the young Weller boys also confided to Dawn that the old man would touch them under their pants in private areas. They did not go into the details but they called Allan Weller the "dirty old man." It was not considered to be a serious problem by the boys. It was almost considered a joke and almost a fact of life in the family.

Her life at the foster home became a "catch as catch can" for the young girl and many of the men that surrounded her.

The only other person Dawn told about her sexual abuse was a relative of her foster mother. She was about twelve when she opened up to the older woman and told her everything.

Dawn recalled that the older lady cried, held her in her arms and they both cried. "Yes, my dear, I know you got a hard life with them," was her comment.

However the woman appears to have done nothing to stop Dawn's troubles. She did not report it to the police or the Social Services Department. So in spite of her confiding in two people, the abuse continued for years after that. The woman's tears were all the comfort or help Dawn ever received from God or man until she was old enough to stop the abuse herself.

In June of 1980, when Dawn was still twelve a social worker wrote in her Child Progress Report:

> Dawn is an attractive girl with short brown hair and blue eyes ... Dawn does not have any emotional problems. She is a very pleasant child who was somewhat shy and quiet in the worker's presence. She seems to be a well adjusted twelve year old.

The worker added that Dawn had a "very close relationship" with her foster parents. It was not entirely untrue.

A curious letter from a temporary social worker to the Regional Director of Social Services is dated August 21, 1980. It reads:

> The above named foster home has been visited four times in the past two months in an attempt to complete the annual foster home review. Mrs. Weller has been absent from the home on each occasion.

> In addition to these regular visits, a worker has phoned Mrs. Weller several times to set up an appointment which would be suitable for both, but has been unable to do so for various reasons.

In July of 1981 when Dawn had just turned fourteen and was being sexually abused by at least four men in her foster family, a social worker, Beverly Eveley, writes:

> Dawn has no apparent emotional or behavioral problems. She is a pleasant friendly girl who was somewhat shy in the worker's presence. She appears happy and content at the Weller home ... Roman Catholic by faith. She attends church regularly ...

> There has been a deep attachment formed between Mr. and Mrs. Weller and Dawn. They consider her their daughter and Dawn considers them her parents and related to them as such. She is receptive to discipline when such is necessary. Dawn is receiving excellent care at the Weller home and is an accepted family member.

Dawn's social workers continued these reports on her circumstances that were so inaccurate and at variance with reality. These reports are so incorrect that they would be ludicrous if the circumstances were different. As it is they are tragic and pathetic.

So Dawn lived out her years from 9 to 16 at the Weller home. She recalls good relationships with her Uncle Pat, who was kind to her. Albert's son David and Levi's son Gary were friends when occasion permitted. Also Albert's wife Alice, who would later be Tammy's foster mother, was a woman Dawn always felt she could trust. In spite of this, she never confided in any of them the story of her sexual relationship with her foster father.

At school she was unable to concentrate on her academics and demonstrated a resentment of school authorities especially as she got older.

"I tried at first. I did good and brought home my report card. But they didn't care. No one was as good as their real kids."

There were often negative remarks aimed at her natural parents, especially her mother, that hurt Dawn. As well, it was pointed out: "You are only a foster kid; you came from nothing and you'll go back to nothing."

Soon Dawn stopped caring.

"In grade six I just wanted to skip off and have a cigarette with my friend Sherry West."

She did not have a memorable relationship with any of her teachers: "They were probably nice, but I didn't trust any adult." And so, she did not confide her problems in a teacher or guidance counsellor.

Although she attended church on Sundays, Dawn did not consider confiding her problems in the local parish priest either.

"We went to church every Sunday, but only because we were forced to. I found it boring."

Dawn was to be the solution to her own problems when she became old enough to stop the abuse for herself. One day when she was in grade eight she was sent home from school because of illness. Her Uncle Pat picked her up at school and dropped her off at her house.

She arrived to find Billy, now twenty years old, playing cards on the coffee table. "Want to play strip poker?" he asked.

"No, I'm home from school because I'm sick."

Ignoring her remarks, Billy took her up off her feet and carried her to his bedroom.

"Stop. Billy, you stop it," she screamed.

He pulled off her clothes and forced her to have sexual intercourse with him. When it was over he let her up but she became very angry at him. Instead of accepting the inevitability of these assaults something clicked in her mind on this occasion like a revelation. Her mind, like a balance scales when too much has been added, turned and tipped irrevocably the other way.

She was fourteen years old, light complexioned and very pretty. She was about 5 foot 2 inches and weighed about 110 pounds. Billy Weller was a big young man, but for some reason Dawn started to fight back.

> I freaked out at him. I remember shouting
> and cursing at him and calling him names.
> Finally, I ran in my room and locked the door.
> That was the last time he touched me.

Perhaps encouraged by this success she soon resisted and ended advances from her foster father, Levi. Fear of her revealing these incidents to the public may have had more to do with the men leaving her alone. Her furious resistance suggested a finality and a refusal to accept it any longer.

On June 9, 1981 Theresa Williams approached the Director of Child Welfare in St. John's through social worker, Rose Hearn. Theresa wanted to know if Dawn, the daughter she had placed in his care, intended for adoption in January, 1974, had indeed been adopted.

It was a reasonable question given the eight year interval. Theresa indicated that she did not want to interfere, or even contact the girl if a successful adoption had occurred. She just wanted to know. She also indicated that if Dawn ever wanted some contact with her natural mother then she would be prepared for any such contact.

On July 8, 1981 a temporary social worker reported to the Regional Director of the Department of Social Services:

> Because of the excellent services such as love and security the Wellers have provided for Dawn and the deep attachment which has been formed, worker recommends that we continue to avail of these services on behalf of Dawn.

The first faint echo of trouble reflected in any social worker's report was in March of 1982. Bonita Rush begins with the usual superficiality:

> Dawn is a very attractive looking girl, quite tall and thin. She dresses stylishly in good taste.... She has been somewhat troubled recently as she feels the Wellers do not care deeply about her.

Rush noted that Dawn was repeating grade eight. No interview was done with her teachers.

Experiencing some problems at the present
time in that Dawn does not want to keep the
rules of the house. Some jealousy between
Dawn and Louise.

Rush knew nothing of the sexual abuse because Dawn did
not know or trust any of her social workers well enough to tell
her. Not only were the social workers responsible for an average
of over one hundred cases at this time, but the same worker
rarely stayed long enough to build up a rapport with the child. In
fact Bonita Rush appears to have been one of the more observant
and empathetic of the workers who dealt with this tragic case.

One would expect Dawn's life to improve considerably after
the termination of the sexual abuse by Levi and Billy. As a foster
father, Levi treated her well in many ways and tried to control
her growing independence as a rebellious teenager. He seemed to
realize that his avenues for sexual fulfilment with her were now
closed and wanted to leave the past in the past. He may have
found another avenue for his paedophilia.

The normal stress and strain of growing up was still on Dawn
William's frail shoulders. She had few supports in her present
life, and little wisdom and emotional stability from her past to
sustain her.

She also had a poor academic career to add to her
frustrations. She solved this problem by ignoring it, "not caring
about it" and avoiding it where possible. Consequently, she
repeated grade eight and grade nine.

She still had the emotional scars of abandonment that foster
children often feel. As well there was the feeling of low self
worth and second rate status in a society full of "real children".
Even though the actual abuse had stopped except for Albert
Weller's occasional groping and fondling, the damage to her self
image was severe.

As a sexual human being she saw herself as a panderer to
other peoples' libidos. She tried to joke, "...the Wellers had
asked for a playmate for their little girl but I was turned into a
playmate for their men."

Dawn turned to an active teenage social life to take her mind off her emotional hurts and family problems. Soon the world of boys was opened to her.

When Dawn became sixteen on July, 5, 1983, her status changed with the Department of Social Services. They would no longer pay her foster parents to maintain her without an extension of foster care being granted.

In July 27, 1983 this extension was granted. The temporary social worker's letter requesting the extension gives an interesting picture of Dawn's life at the time of her sixteenth birthday:

> She has a close relationship with all family members, especially Mrs. Weller. Dawn failed her grade 9 this year and will be returning to school to repeat the grade. Mrs. Weller encourages Dawn with her education but Dawn had other interests that she felt were more important. She says she now realizes how important it is to work hard in school and she intends to get more serious about her school work in September.

In fact Dawn had no such intentions. Her "close relationship with all family members" was in four cases sexually abusive. The letter must stand as a rarely parallelled example of professional wishful thinking. It also gets high marks for missing an abusive family situation and reporting an inaccurate picture to the director of Child Welfare.

This letter seems oddly at variance with the Child Progress Report done that same month by the same department:

> Dawn failed her grade 9 this year and is not really interested in school. Mrs. Weller was quite upset and insists Dawn will study harder this year ... she is very popular with boys. She is developed for her age and considers herself much older.

The bitter-sweet world of teenage romance had already opened its rosy door for Dawn. A very attractive girl, she met

John Hibbs at a teenage dance in Baywood when she was sixteen. He was nineteen and sported a tattoo on each arm. John worked as a gas station attendant as he had dropped out of school. He had driven up from Walcove with a carload of his buddies to attend the dance.

No stranger to the beer bottle, cigarette and marijuana joint, John cut an attractive figure to the sixteen year old Dawn. He wore Levis, and a leather jacket. He had short curly hair and big blue eyes.

His persona was a rejection of the hypocritical adult society in which Dawn lived. She was being sexually abused by the males in her foster family all week long, and when Sunday morning came she was bundled off to church. In her heart she hated the pretension to holiness and the hidden sexuality denied by all. She had never thought it all through in a logical manner but she instinctively rejected the pretension, the lies and the deception. On the surface her life was fine but inside it was indeed like the tomb, white on the outside but inside "full of dead men's bones."

Here, at last, was the physical embodiment of that rejection. John Hibbs made no false pretence of his sexuality and she recognized an honesty in him. He spoke more truth with one of his tattoos than she had yet heard.

To add to the attraction, he was quiet and shy. Every father's nightmare, John was Dawn's dream come true. Soon they were dating steadily.

In the Weller home Dawn was having trouble with the house rules. She wanted to stay out later in the nights than the Wellers thought appropriate for a sixteen year old girl. She wanted to be treated like their natural daughter, Louise, who was four years older. This may have reflected Dawn's wish to be a natural daughter like Louise.

Problems escalated and soon the late hours were combined with problem drinking. Dawn rejected the Weller's attempt to control her hours outside the home, which were usually spent in the company of her boyfriend, John Hibbs. She had confided to John that there had been sexual assault from her foster father; she did not tell him about Billy or Albert or the grandfather.

Things came to a head on a Friday night in November of 1983. It was actually three o'clock Saturday morning when Dawn arrived home, drunk. She had been attending a dance with her boyfriend. An irate Mary Weller demanded an explanation and angry words were exchanged. The upshot was that Mrs. Weller announced that Dawn's dance card would be severely restricted for the remainder of the winter.

The next morning Dawn packed her bags and moved out with the help of her boyfriend. Mrs. Weller admitted that these problems had been ongoing for some time but she had not informed the social worker. Mrs. Weller saw the problem as being Dawn's drinking, lying and taking benefits for granted.

It was at this time, in the Hibbs family basement in Walcove that Dawn claims to have blurted out to the social worker that she was being sexually abused in the Weller foster home. Edith Decker had come to retrieve the rebellious teenager. Dawn says she told Edith the following: "I'm not going back to sexual abuse."

Dawn remembers that Edith went completely silent for a few moments and finally said, "You stay here and I'll be right back for you." She then left, perhaps for her office a few kilometres distant in Shipley.

When she returned the elusive Dawn had fled, but not back to the Weller household.

Dawn then went to live at Presentation House for a few weeks until the matter was worked out. This is a transitional house run by the Presentation Order of nuns for children on their way to and from foster homes. She has fond memories of the house and remembers talking with at least one of the nuns but she did not confide about her sexual abuse. She found life there very strict and she found occasion to dislike one of the nuns intensely.

An analysis of the problem by social worker, Edith Decker, shows just how little the professional person assigned to Dawn's case understood the real problem. Edith had concluded that Dawn's problems stemmed from her past and not her present situation.

What is more significant, the social worker appears to have

misunderstood, ignored or forgotten Dawn's alleged revelation about sexual abuse:

> Dawn is a very disturbed and confused teenager. She has very much difficulty in accepting her past, her mother's rejection.

Edith was to be a pivotal player in another tragedy when Tammy King arrived at the house next door to Dawn's three years later. Dawn's memories of Edith are all unpleasant. No doubt, sixteen year old Dawn presented a challenge to any social worker.

Dawn moved out of the Weller household in a car driven by John's buddy. The grim faced girl and the two arrogantly casual young men sped away and left the Weller home and its problems in their dust.

But problems, like tattoos, cannot easily be removed. As Dawn left the Weller home she carried more baggage than her few suitcases. With Dawn came much psychological "baggage".

Unlike John Hibbs, Dawn's tattoos were deeper and cut into her inner self where only she could see and feel them. The soreness of John's soon eased, but Dawn's ached eternally at the touch. The prick of each needle and dye were etched deeply into her at a soft, tender level of self that few people really understand.

On November 22, 1983 Dawn was returned to her natural mother, Theresa, after almost ten years of care by the Director of Child Welfare. There was much emotion and genuine love between them. There were lost years to try and regain. The reunion started with much promise.

Theresa must have noticed a great difference in the girl she turned over to the Child Welfare Division in 1974 and the girl she got back in 1983. The blond-headed, seven-year-old, full of fresh innocence and love was gone forever. The naive desire to be accepted and to please was replaced by another set of feelings and values.

This new incarnation was a jaundiced sixteen year old with every reason to be suspicious of this life and its inhabitants. This new one was jarringly familiar with alcohol, cigarettes and other stimulants. This one had a tattooed boyfriend.

One is reminded of Stokley Charmichael's "chickens coming home to roost."

It would be fair to say that once again Theresa was not ready for the experience of Dawn. Theresa was now 34 years old with problems of her own. She and Dean Smith had divorced soon after Dawn had left for the Wellers. The three boys of that marriage and another boy from her second marriage all lived with her and her second husband, Walter Reese.

By now Theresa was prone to depression and frequent crying. The demons of the past had not been exorcised but rather they had moved with Theresa to a new venue and more demons had joined them. Dawn did not tell her mother about sexual abuse at the Weller home, but she did tell her Mom's sister in law. Somehow the woman contacted the Wellers and Dawn remembers nothing but trouble resulting.

The arrangement was impossible for the people involved and by January 24, 1984 Dawn was back at the Weller's house in Deep Harbour. She was to remain there only three months, but during that time three important events occurred:

A month after she arrived she became pregnant. Not an unpredictable event given the circumstances of her lifestyle with boyfriend, John Hibbs. She had been given no birth control counselling, either at the foster home, the school, or Presentation House. These institutions did not allow birth control even for adults.

Although there were medical clinics, and nurses and doctors available to her, Dawn did not trust their services in her sexual life. She did not confide in them about the sexual abuse at her foster home or her sexual activity with her boyfriend. She was under the impression that the doctors and nurses would reveal these matters to her foster parents, and that she would not have confidentiality when she talked to a doctor. Many high school students today are under this same impression. This confusion is occasioned by unnecessarily vagueness on the matter.

Two months after she arrived she claims to have been sexually assaulted by Levi's brother Albert. He was visiting the house one day when she was there alone. He grabbed her and pushed his hand down inside her pants. He touched her but it did not progress to sexual intercourse. According to Dawn, this was not the only time he had done this but as events transpired it was the last.

Three months after she arrived she moved to Calgary, Alberta to be with her boyfriend.

In spite of these events the social workers' reports proceed, blithely ignorant of reality. Edith Decker writes as if she were describing a different child in a different home, perhaps in a fairy tale:

> Dawn is of the Roman Catholic faith and attends church regularly.... No problems in this area (attachment, discipline, problems). The foster parents are very attached to Dawn. She is treated as their own and given what she wants. A good relationship exists with the natural children. Her plans for the future are to remain in this home and to continue her education.

Four days after Dawn left for Calgary, the social worker informed the Director of Child Welfare that the Wellers were closing out their foster home. "The Wellers have been foster parents since 1973 and have provided excellent services to our department."

This is rather a glowing accolade when contrasted with the fact that by 1990 four charges of sexual assault had been laid against the Weller men in her foster family.

Dawn flew to Calgary and John was at the airport to meet her. For with his tattoos and grade school education and lack of material prospects, he loved her. An airline ticket from St. John's to Calgary was a significant part of his budget, considering his expenditures on beer, cigarettes and drugs. But he cared for her and he wanted her with him, so he sent her the ticket.

Dawn was driven to the airport by her foster parents, Levi and Mary Weller. Both were discouraging her from leaving. Dismissing their advice, which, in this case, may have been quite good, she followed her heart westward to Calgary. As the plane left St. John's Airport, Dawn felt the asphalt fall away beneath her feet. She hoped the problems she faced on the ground would fall away with it. If only!

But inside her the baby grew, and in her heart the emotional hurts of her past grew too.

Her mother's turning her over to the Social Services Department plagued her with feelings of unworthiness and rejection. She longed for a steady mother figure and she longed for emotional stability in her life.

The sexual abuse at the Weller foster home had hurt Dawn deeply. Sexuality was cheapened and her self concept was further deflated. She saw her sexuality as a convenience for others and found it unfulfilling for her.

She responded to these hurts with drinking, outbursts of anger, and verbal and emotional abuse against those around her. She did not understand her anger and tried to forget about the abuse and abandonment. She avoided dealing with these painful memories from her past.

But these hurts soon take on a life of their own and in time they grow into what we are as human beings.

Dawn tried to ignore them as they hung like rotting albatrosses around her thin neck. Their putrid stench filled her life with years of misery, depression, and failed relationships. Dawn could never understand why.

As often happens in this life, we seem to leave one set of problems only to face another set. Life in Calgary was not as good as she had hoped. Although John was always there for her and they lived with his sister and her husband, they did not have a room or even a bed; so they slept on couch, floor, mattress depending on circumstances and other visitors in the house. Dawn was advancing in her pregnancy and was frequently sick. Their hosts were doing quite a lot of drugs and although Dawn was welcome, she was not contented.

The big obstacle was health care. With the baby's arrival fast approaching Dawn discovered that she would have problems transferring to the Alberta medical care service. The bureaucratic problems could be ironed out in a matter of time, but with the baby coming, Dawn did not have time. From a financial point of view it seemed to her that she must return to Newfoundland.

On June 7, 1984, she reluctantly returned to St. John's, Newfoundland to depend once again on the auspices of the Department of Social Services. She had no place to stay so she was put up at Emmanuel House in the city. It was a temporary transition house for young people with a variety of problems.

It was a difficult time for her. She was eating poorly and was frequently depressed. On August 7th she moved into Elizabeth House, a home for unwed mothers where she was treated well by the husband and wife team that ran it. There her baby Laura, was born on September 10, 1984.

Around this time Dawn informed social worker Gladys Walker that she had been sexually assaulted at the Wellers. As Edith Decker writes to the Director of Child Welfare in 1985:

> ... in 1984 after much unrest, Dawn emplied that Mr. Weller had sexually abused her. This implication was made to Gladys Walker at St. John's Centre. No action was taken in this because Dawn did not state clearly around this matter.

Edith Decker's misspelling and incorrect use of language are not the only errors in her letter to the Director. The actual report, a nineteen page social history of Dawn, written by a social worker in September, 1984, reveals quite a different story from Edith's letter. It reads in part:

> Dawn stated that as she went through adolescent years her foster father and foster brother had sexually abused her on a number of occasions. Dawn said that her foster father had never had sexual intercourse with her but that he used to touch her in 'private areas.' Her foster brother, however, had forced himself upon her at one time.
>
> Dawn said that she was very scared at this time and was also afraid of losing her

> only family. It has only been recently that any
> of this has been mentioned by Dawn, and
> therefore none of it has been investigated.
> Dawn does not want to cause problems
> between her foster parents and feels guilty
> about what has happened.

That was written in September, 1984. It is apparent that Dawn had not "implied" or talked around the matter of her sexual abuse at the hands of the Weller men. She stated it clearly and accurately. She told social worker, Gladys Walker, about the abuse and she named the men who had abused her. Edith appears to have seriously missed the mark in her letter to the director in the following year.

The next chapter will show that at this time, September, 1984, the second girl in this book, Ann Wicks, was being abused by Levi Weller's brother Albert Weller and others at her foster home, next door. This was over two years before Tammy and Maggie King would innocently arrive at the Weller's home from Deer Lake. So much harm could have been averted if Dawn's clear allegations in 1984 to the social workers had been acted upon.

Once again, nothing was done.

The social worker who looked over her desk at the pregnant Dawn in 1984 saw a picture very similar to the one seen by Theresa's social worker in 1967. In fact, there is a mention in the report of the striking physical similarity between the mother, Theresa, and the daughter, Dawn. There was the similar age, hair, eyes, height, and weight.

But the similarities did not end there. Both were pregnant without stable relationships. Both were distraught and overwhelmed by circumstances. Both were worried about their future and the future of their unborn child. Both reluctantly placed the child for adoption, hopeful of a better future. Through Dawn's baby, Laura, the endless cycle was continued to the next generation.

CHAPTER 6

ANN WICKS

He does not break the crushed reed nor
snuff out the wavering flame.

Isaiah 42:3

On February 25, 1981, Levi Weller's brother, Albert Weller and his wife Alice were given their license to operate a foster home in Deep Harbour. This was the home to which Tammy King and her younger sister Maggie would be delivered by the provincial Department of Social Services five years later.

Initially two young brothers were placed with Albert and Alice, but the match did not work. The brothers lasted there only one day because, in the quietly bureaucratic words of the Social Services Department, "the boys were exhibiting a strong reaction to placement and the family could not cope." Between those fifteen words, is painted a human tragedy of frenzied and painful emotions.

Two years later on March 24, 1983 Ann Wicks arrived at the Albert Weller home. She had just come from another foster home placement of thirteen years.

Ann was born on July 31, 1967, in the same month and year as Dawn Williams. In 1983 she was fifteen years old and had her own litany of bad experiences like Dawn and many other foster children. Unfortunately Ann was born a victim of nature, not just of man, in that she had cystic fibrosis, a degenerative lung disease. Ann took this disease in her stride and has continued to do so throughout her life.

Ann had been in the care of the Director of Social Services since she was three years old in 1971. She had then been placed in a rural home for special needs children affiliated with Exon House in St. John's.

The home was run by a former nursing assistant and her husband. Their original license to care for one child had gradually been increased to nine children. This showed the high regard in which the establishment was held by the Social Services Department. The home took much strain off the Department in the handling of some of its more problematic, special needs children.

Ann was the first child in this home. Although she had cystic fibrosis, she was not incapacitated and as she got older she was expected to help with the running of the home.

When she reached her early teens the number of children at the home had increased and with it the workload. Ann was expected to wash the dishes, clean the floors, make the beds, and supervise the other children when the foster parents were absent. She was a valuable asset to them as baby sitter and general factotum.

Like many teenagers, she began to object to what was becoming an unmanageable workload. She had her own school work to complete and a growing social life that included young friends her own age.

Her objections fell on deaf ears and her foster mother sought to enforce obedience with physical beatings, sometimes with a sawn off broom handle. This continued until around the time Ann was fifteen.

Ann made periodic trips to the Janeway Children's Hospital in St. John's for medical check ups. She also attended cystic fibrosis camps during the summer. It was there that she first complained about physical abuse at the foster home.

She developed friendships with nurses at the Janeway and workers at the summer camp. One of these nurses was Alicia Rollings who would play a larger role in Ann's story later on.

Soon after this, Ann was keeping a diary, chronicling the physical beatings by her foster mother. She complained and social workers investigated.

The social workers were not sympathetic to Ann's complaints for a number of reasons. They did not want to lose a very valuable home which was caring for special needs children. Also, they had helped the foster mother secure extra funding for the home and felt a psychological ownership of the establishment. If the complaints of physical abuse were substantiated, and the home were closed by the Department, what would they do with the nine special needs children already there?

There was probably another purely psychological dimension to this problem. The social workers may have felt that the staff at the Janeway were meddling in their territory. They were unsympathetic to Ann's complaints and one social worker was, as Justice Hughes pointed out in his Royal Commission, openly hostile. This worker wrote long letters to headquarters describing the situation as springing from Ann's "mischief making."

No charges were then laid against the foster mother, but Ann was moved to another foster home at the request of the foster parents. Her school year was interrupted, for the move was not delayed until the end of the school year. In this abrupt manner she came to the home of Albert Weller. It now appears from Ann's most recent statement to the Supreme Court that she was being abused physically, emotionally and sexually at this first foster home. Like many others, she maintained this bitter secrecy for years.

There were many things the sixteen year old liked about the home. Albert's son, David, two years younger than Ann, was friendly in a quiet, brotherly way. Alice, Albert' wife, was sincere and empathetic. Both David and Alice were to remain true friends to Ann through her troubles.

Alice Weller, especially, was good to all the girls who were foster children at the Albert Weller home. Even Dawn Williams, who lived next door in the Levi Weller home, came to trust and love her. Alice treated Ann like her own daughter. She gave the unselfish love and caring that these girls lacked and, more than most, needed.

Ann had an enjoyable first summer in Deep Harbour in 1983. She got to know the family and the extended family of Wellers who lived nearby.

She met Dawn Williams who had been sexually abused next door, but felt they had little in common except for the fact that they were both foster children. Dawn did not tell Ann about her secret sexual life with the Weller men. Ann did not buddy around with Dawn's friends. She did not toke or drink, and her cystic fibrosis as well as her conservative attitude led her away from cigarettes.

Ann started the tenth grade in September of 1983 at the Catholic central high school for the area, Balarri High. A very pleasant, blond-haired girl, Ann was doing well in school and was much more positive towards authority than Dawn. She enjoyed school and was respectful to her teachers whom she genuinely liked.

She seemed to be adjusting well in her new home. Albert treated her well at first. He was kind and considerate, often taking time to chat with her, listening to her thoughts and sometimes offering his own.

After she had been in the home for about ten months, in January, 1984, Albert Weller began directing sexual behaviour towards her. It began as innocent pranks, pinching, or tickling. He would lift the back of her shirt as she passed or flip a beer cap down her top. It was always done in a playful, joking manner. It always took place in the home and later only when there was no one in the room.

At first Ann was not upset by his behaviour. She had seen him do the same to other women in the house like Alice and her sister. He would do it as if it were a natural part of playing around. Ann would be passing by him in the kitchen and he would reach out and pinch her on the bum.

As he got to know Ann and her level of tolerance for his behaviour the sexual intent intensified. That winter he began touching her breasts as well as her bum on the outside of her clothing. He would let his fingers linger a little longer than if it were still a joke. By winter of 1984 the light pinching had progressed to touching and feeling.

In the evenings Alice would often go out, to bingo or visiting. If David were not at home, Ann and Albert would watch television together. Albert would sit in the arm chair and Ann would sit on the chesterfield close beside it.

One evening that winter the two were watching television when there was no one else home. Outside the snow was a blanket that covered the frozen paths of summer and the fields that led down to the ponds. Dark ice, thick and strong groaned under the snow where happy kids had waded and splashed in August. Spruce trees dozed shoulder to shoulder under this soft, white blanket.

Tire tracks in the snow led out of the yard to the road where the bingo bus had just collected avid supporters like Alice Weller. An occasional car sloshed through the snowy road by Albert Weller's house.

The living room was lit with the blue glow from the television. The only sound was the program being broadcast.

Albert reached over, slipped his hand inside her tee-shirt and touched her full breast. Ann leaned away but continued to watch television. She placed her hands across her breasts to stop his groping. He leaned toward her on the edge of his chair as she leaned away as far as she could and still see the television. She did not speak.

"It's all right," he coaxed. "There's nothing wrong with it."

Now he had his fingers under her bra and was stroking her breasts. She said nothing. May be there was nothing wrong with it. It was uncomfortable at first but strangely exciting. She did not get up and leave the room or even the chesterfield.

"Come on. It's OK." He continued to stroke her breast.

This strange family pose continued as the television covered the two participants in an eerie blue glow and the "Wheel of Fortune" rolled surreally on the TV screen.

Albert continued touching the girl until his sexual intentions had been satisfied. These incidents occurred sometimes three or four times a week, always in the evenings while the two of them were watching television. Sometimes David would be at home in his room with the door closed.

During the winter and spring of 1983 Ann and David took

the school bus to Balarri Central High. Ann was seen as a pleasant student who applied herself to her work. She lacked the worldly wisdom of Dawn Williams and, unlike Dawn, she succeeded at her studies. Her cystic fibrosis was still a problem and sometimes caused her to be ill. She gave no observable indication of her sexual involvement with her foster father many nights of the week.

The Social Services Department too were unaware of Ann's plight at home. The regular visits by the worker were infrequent and often done by a student replacement. A different worker would sometimes appear at the house from one visit to the next. Ann said, "At my first home I didn't know who my social worker was." Ann never got to know her social worker, Edith Decker, in any meaningful way while she was at the Weller home. As with other social workers, Edith's severe caseload made familiarity with her many clients impossible.

Another problem was that the social worker rarely spoke to Ann alone. There was always one of the foster parents present. This problem was referenced by author Derek O'Brien in the tragic biography of his life as a foster child in Newfoundland:

> As far as I'm concerned, to the welfare department, we were just a number on a file, and with that number came payment for our care. The welfare officers would come every now and then and have a cup of tea with the foster parents, smile a lot, and go on to the next house. They never looked for any sign that something was wrong. When we lived at Mrs. Dinns's she would dress us up in new clothes, stand us up and wait for the welfare officer to come. She would also warn us not to say a word when we were asked questions.

Ann was not even present in the home when some of these semi-annual reports were being done. She was in school and did not see the worker. There was no basis for trust or even personal contact developed by the social workers of the Department of

Social Services, Child Welfare Division.

During the three years of her sexual abuse at the Weller home, Ann did not confide in the social workers who turned up at the home. She was scared of what would happen to her if she told, and she did not know or trust them sufficiently to place her life in their hands.

The workers reported that nothing was amiss, and that the child was doing well at the home. This was similar to the inaccuracies reported by the same people on the Levi Weller foster home next door where Dawn Williams had been sexually abused for six years by four different men.

That same winter and spring the intensity and variety of the sexual abuse increased. There was no physical beating or violence involved. Albert insinuated himself into the sexual activity with a mixture of psychological devices.

Why did Ann allow it to happen? There was always the threat of a group home. Also there was the charge of mischief-making against Ann if their activity became known. As well, Ann loved Alice and did not want to hurt her foster mother or lose that friendship. Finally, there was the home and the security of a family, even if there was one repulsive dimension, the sexual abuse by her foster father.

Although she did not tell anyone what she and Albert Weller were doing, she did change her attitude towards him. She came to dislike him very much and argue with him over other matters. She bickered with him and ignored him often. They argued about seemingly unrelated things like her coming home from babysitting on a Saturday to cleaning up her room. The tension and antagonism between them escalated up to the final, extended sexual assault in June of 1985.

In the evenings the sexual activity continued between Albert and Ann several times a week. The touching became more intense as he moved from her breasts to the vaginal area of her body. He took Ann's hand and placed it on his crotch. He would open his pants and take out his penis. She would take it in her hand and continue until he was satisfied.

Often Alice and David would be at home and in bed when this was occurring. It would be around eleven or eleven thirty at night in the living room with the television on. He would now move to the couch with her and touch her. She would not cry out nor would she run to her room.

Soon Albert was coming into her bedroom when no one else was at home. At least twice Ann admitted to performing oral sex on him. During 1985 the sexual activity continued and escalated. One morning before the summer of 1985, just before Ann's June exams, Alice had left the house early and David was not at home. Albert came into Ann's bedroom while she was still in bed. He was naked except for his underwear. He came to the bed and leaned over her. She was still covered with blankets which he put aside.

She closed her eyes and pretended to be asleep. He said nothing, but soon she could feel him touching her breast. She rolled over away from him but he continued to touch her body. Ann was wearing a knee length night gown and underwear. Albert pushed up the night dress and began to touch her vaginal area. This continued for a time in a manner that had happened before. But soon Ann was aware that this time he intended to go farther than ever before.

"Stop it," she murmured, in a manner that he had always ignored.

"It's OK, Ann. There's nothing wrong with it."

He pulled off her underwear and got on top of her. He said, "Now I'm going to get your cherry."

"What do you mean?"

"I'm going to have sex with you."

She told him to stop it and pushed her legs together but he forced them apart.

"I don't want to get pregnant," Ann pleaded.

"You won't get pregnant. I'll take it out before I come."

He continued and finally inserted his penis, clearly against the struggling girl's wishes.

"No. no."

When he was finished he got up off the bed.

"Make sure you never tell Alice or anyone else."

"Why shouldn't I tell them?"

"Because no one will believe you. In their eyes it will be all your fault for causing trouble, just like they said in your first foster home."

Albert then went into the bathroom and cleaned up. Ann waited in her room and cried. When he came out she went in and tried to wash her soiled body and clean away her memory of the event.

That summer she went back to her home in Catalina and stayed with her natural father. It was there that she celebrated her 18th birthday. She returned to the Weller foster home for the school year which began in September, 1985. This was to be her graduating year from high school and her last year at the foster home.

Things were different between her and Albert. She kept away from him by visiting Alice's sister in Baywood and staying all week. There she had a welcomed friend in Alice's niece. She returned to the Weller home only when necessary, for example, on weekends. The family in Baywood who hosted the pleasant young woman were unknowingly delivering her from an abusive situation in her foster home.

In this manner she managed to elude the sexual advances of Albert Weller for her final year in his care and control.

Three years later in court, Ann was asked by a Crown prosecutor why she had remained silent during these many nights of sexual abuse when others, like Alice, were often in the house at the time. She answered:

"Because I didn't want Alice to hear what was going on. I knew there would be a fuss. I didn't want her to know because I didn't want to hurt her. I loved Alice. She was what I wanted as a mother. I never had a mother and she was my idol as a mother. And I didn't want to hurt her. So I just took it."

At Albert's trial in 1989, she was asked why she had permitted the abuse. She answered:

> Because all my life I have ... done what other people have told me. If I didn't obey I have been punished for it and I was just too scared. I didn't know any difference. I was never told the difference.

Like Dawn Williams, she felt that she was in no position to set demands upon her foster home. There was an unspoken and sometimes spoken feeling of being "beholden" to any home that would take her. At least she was not in a dreaded group home. She felt that she was "only" a foster child and was lucky to be with a "real" family.

If she complained of the sexual abuse, she would be moved somewhere else with more strangers, while Albert would continue his life untouched. She would lose her home, friends, Alice, and her reputation. That was the reality of life for a foster child in 1985. Within three years she was to change much of that for herself but for other foster children in Newfoundland little has changed.

In the summer of 1986 Ann went to summer camp for cystic fibrosis patients run by the Janeway Hospital. Something she did there was to change her life and raise a brave banner for many other foster children.

On the last night of the camp Ann was in a state of turmoil. She stood in the night outside the door of nurse Alicia Rollings. She did not know what to do with her life. The week in camp with other cystic fibrosis kids reminded her that there was no cure for her disease. There were few kids as old as she who were still alive.

She knew that the cystic fibrosis was killing her. Five years before, the average life expectancy would be mid-teen years. Advances in research and improvements in medication meant that by 1986 the life expectancy reached into the late teens or twenties. In July of 1986 she was nineteen. Of course, some patients lived even longer. The then oldest known surviving person in the province was thirty four.

Also troubling her was the sexual abuse at the foster home. She had avoided it with Albert since the previous June, but it was still a threat while she lived at the Weller home. As well, her emotional state was troubled by guilt and feelings of evil that bothered her in dreams and flashbacks. Yet she loved Alice, David, school, her chums and generally loved her life at the home.

With a troubled heart the teenager knocked on the door of

camp nurse, Alicia Rollings. She had known Alicia since 1982 when they had met at the Janeway Children's Hospital. Every summer since then they had met at Cystic Fibrosis Camp.

A sympathetic Rollings listened to the girl's story. Ann was perturbed about a decision she had to make. Should she go back to live with her father in Catalina, or should she return to the Weller foster home? Soon Ann reluctantly confided to the nurse the real reason for her hesitation to return to her foster home.

Ann told Rollings that she had been sexually abused by Albert Weller. This revelation would later set in motion a series of events that were to change the lives of many foster children. Ann helped develop an awareness of the problem. But unfortunately there was an immediate two year delay in these events, during which time much harm was set in motion.

The results of Ann's disclosure were not immediately evident. Like Hamlet's ghost, Ann unfortunately exacted a pledge from Rollings to reveal to no one what she had been told.

Rollings was bound by law to immediately inform the Director of Child Welfare of what she knew, but she did not do so. On the next day she did tell the Cystic Fibrosis coordinator, Ruth Howse, another nurse at the camp.

Alicia Rollings took a special interest in Ann, who returned to her father's home in Catalina. Rollings visited her there and spent a few days. There was an exchange of letters, Christmas cards, and when Ann was in St. John's for clinic visits at the Janeway, she stayed at Rollings's house overnight.

For two years Alicia kept Ann's secret and mentioned the revelation of abuse to no one else. Rollings may have assumed that the Cystic Fibrosis camp coordinator would have contacted the authorities. If not, she could have reasoned, her promise to Ann would be kept.

For Tammy King, however, the plot had complicated itself much more than that by 1988. If the report had occurred in 1986 when Ann first made the allegation it may have saved Tammy's life. But, as we shall see in the next chapter, by the late summer of 1988 there were many new circumstances in Tammy's life.

CHAPTER 7

WELCOME TO DEEP HARBOUR

Halloween 1986

Deep Harbour is a ruggedly attractive community situated a pleasant drive from St. John's, the capital. It is inhabited by some of the finest people one will ever meet on the island of Newfoundland.

The local temperament is quiet but not sullen. They are a people whose generations have struggled with a harsh and humbling competitor, the sea, for over three hundred years.

Deep Harbour was a fishing station for French, Basques and English fishermen since the time of Shakespeare. It was first settled by Europeans in the sixteen hundreds.

Another important factor in the history of Deep Harbour is its Roman Catholic faith. A few Catholic families like the Fureys, Hawcos and the Lacoeurs are of French Huguenot extraction who came from the Channel Islands.

The vast majority of families are of Irish descent. Kennedy, Dobbin, Cleary, Costigan, Flynn, Hickey, Moore, Joy, Kelly, and Wall are names that could as easily be read from the telephone directory of Wexford or Dublin. Practically all families in Deep Harbour are Catholic.

To understand the people of Deep Harbour one must first understand their Irish Catholicism. They were and still are a minority in a predominantly protestant province, and in centuries of sectarian strife they became fiercely defensive. Even today in an increasingly ecumenical and often humanistic world, they identify strongly with their religion.

In 1755, a resident of Deep Harbour, was found guilty by the courts of having allowed a priest to celebrate mass in his fishing store. He was sentenced to destroy the building, sell all his possessions and was fined fifty pounds, in those days an exorbitant amount. Other residents were similarly fined or effectively banished. In those days Catholics were often forced to celebrate Mass in the woods. The altar cloth was draped over a suitable flat rock called a "Mass rock." Whatever the cost, it was gladly paid to preserve their Roman Catholic faith.

This was only sixty-four years after the defeat of the Catholic forces at the Battle of the Boyne, an event still celebrated every year by Orangemen in the area. The "Penal Laws" in the 1700's sought to control Catholics as a social force. As writer, Cyril Byrne, explains those times:

> Catholics were barred from holding any public office; they could not operate schools; they could not sit in Parliament, nor own property or lease it except for ridiculously short periods of time, and, as a final humiliating gesture in an age when the man on horseback symbolized the gentry ...no Catholic could own a horse of greater value than five pounds.

Their descendants endured, often illegally, and were not driven out by the harsh sea nor the equally harsh British government. They recently celebrated with great joy the 125th anniversary of their parish, the appropriately named Deep Harbour.

Their religion was a unifying strength. Over the centuries the role of the church in people's lives has declined. But old traditions change slowly. One such tradition that still exists is the puritanical streak that applies to human sexuality. Of course, this is not exclusive to Irish Catholics.

In Irish Catholic communities, no evil is considered quite as bad as a sexual evil. From the point of view of the official Catholic Church, the function of sex is for procreation, not for pleasure. Its enjoyment is further curtailed by church regulations governing birth control. Celibacy is seen as the most highly spiritual of human sexual conditions and is mandatory for priests, brothers and nuns.

Senior crown prosecutor Frank Gronich was to play a prominent role in the investigation into Tammy's death. He later reflected on the social background to her tragedy:

> Catholics, especially Irish Catholics, have some kind of idea that sex is bad. Any pleasure from sexuality is somehow sinful. I think that had an impact upon the society in the area. I think the priests instilled the wrong principles of sexuality into the population.

The official church views on sexuality may be largely ignored by Catholics in their private lives but people still respect many of the religious traditions of their church.

There is love for the institution of the church in most Irish Catholic communities, especially among older people. This love is felt like love of family or children, who, even if they do wrong, must not be criticized by outsiders.

Social approval of the church is manifested in parish fund raisers like garden parties in summer and bingo throughout the year, church attendance on Sunday and donations of money. It also is manifested in support for the church-run denominational school system. Many people in Deep Harbour support all the above.

It is against this background that we must see the revelations of sex crimes in Newfoundland that began to burst like mortar shells on these people in the last two years of the 1980's.

Also against this background came the stories of sex crimes by some men of the Weller family of Deep Harbour. This is the background of Tammy's story because human sexuality is very much part of her story. Her grief was mainly caused by our profound discomfort in openly discussing sexual topics, our silence. What a high price we pay each year for our false modesty, propriety and correctness. What a high price our children pay each year in sexual ignorance, unwanted pregnancy, guilt and venereal diseases. This is is the complex social and psychological cloak of secrecy that allows sexual victimization to continue. This can and does occur in other societies and other religions where frank discussion of human sexuality is taboo or restricted.

Tammy King, age fourteen, and her sister Maggie, age twelve, arrived in Deep Harbour in late October, 1986. In the Catholic lexicon of celebrations October 31 is the Eve of All Saints' Day, All Hallows' Eve, or "Halloween." In the old Celtic calendar of the Irish tribes before Christianity, it was the last day of the year and the night of all the witches.

The summer weather was already gone from Deep Harbour. Squalls of autumn wind tossed the early leaves around the gravel lane leading up to Albert Weller's little bungalow.

There were lots of trees; not big and tall like west coast timber. These were short and sturdy, reflecting a shorter growing season and thinner soil of the east coast of the island.

Most of them were conifers - spruce and fir. A large pond lay over a nearby hill. The dirt driveway that led to Albert Weller's House was concealed from the main road by spruce trees bunched thickly together.

To the girls it was as barren and bleak a prospect as they had ever seen. There were fewer houses than in Deer Lake, no shopping centres, almost no businesses, less traffic. There were few people and no kids to be seen when they arrived. Maggie said, "When we got there we looked around and me and Tammy just looked at each other because the place seemed so isolated."

Tammy appeared to have been shocked and numbed by the experience of being moved from her Deer Lake foster home. She wrote her father from the Albert Weller foster home on November 24th, 1986. The top of the letter is decorated with two large hearts and the words in large block letters "I WILL ALWAYS LOVE YOU", much like one would find on a tombstone of Victorian vintage.

It is the most revealing of all her twenty letters. In it she lets her feelings be known to her father and reveals herself as in no other letter. Perhaps because the letters were free from adult scrutiny and for the first time she could write her real thoughts. Also, because she had just experienced an uprooting that was especially traumatic for her. She wrote him from Deep Harbour.

November 24,1986

Dear Dad:

I am really sorry if I upset you Sunday. We were just told that Rita never wanted us to write or call because it was better ... I don't know why Rita told us she wanted us to write her and gave us an envelope and to tell her all about the trip out here. We even called her collect that day and she called twice afterwards to talk to Alice (Weller) but not to us.

It was a real upset to me because I was there since I was 8 years old. As far as I was concerned she was my mother.

I don't know why we were put there if that's what was going to happen. Get attached to someone then they kick you out.

That's what I hate about being a foster child. They can threaten you and say anything because they're not worried about what happens as long as it's not their own child.

They all think it is only a stranger and they don't even have to take us into their homes but all they say is that we should be grateful for that. I am grateful for that but it is pretty hard to live with someone when you're worried what's going to happen -Do they want us to get out? or Do they like us? These are questions I often wonder about ...

> I am very sad to hear this about Rita but
> I have to accept it. But I never loved my real
> mother compared to how much ...I loved Rita.

The letter 'd' in the second last word was firmly written over several times, and seems to have been added later. She had first written, "I love Rita."

On the last page was a note:

> Tell Audrey and Uncle Peter if you see
> them before me that I really appreciate
> everything they are doing for me and Maggie
> and I thank you too Dad.

> Give this note to them please. See you
> Saturday. I love you Dad and I hope you will
> always want to see us.

Audrey:

> Thank you Aunt Audrey and Uncle Peter
> for coming out for us. I really appreciate it and
> I love you. You and Dad are the only family I
> have. I use to think I had a family in Deer
> Lake who loved me just as much ... but I was
> wrong. I know now that you, Aunt Audrey
> have been and are the closest person to a
> mother to me. So I love you for everything
> you have done. I don't know what I would do
> without you. I would like to thank you for the
> Love, Tammy.

There followed three hearts drawn in red beside the word "THANKS". Audrey never received the note.

The cold north east winds of an early Newfoundland winter were blowing by October of 1986 when Tammy arrived in Deep Harbour. Racing in from the North Atlantic the north easterlies pushed aside the modest winds of autumn, the westerlies, from the land. These westerlies came from the interior of the island, perhaps from as far west as Deer Lake. They were swept out to sea at Deep Harbour.

Social worker, Don Evans drove up to the Weller house at about 2:30 in the afternoon. Alice and Albert were there to welcome their two new foster children. Alice invited them into the house, Don's wife and child stayed in the car. Introductions were exchanged and Don explained that he had to leave.

"What? You're not going yet, are you?" asked Maggie.

"Yes, I've got to go now," answered the social worker.

Maggie watched Don go through the door and with him went her last link with Deer Lake and what she considered home. She looked at Tammy, standing awkwardly in the strange kitchen.

"I felt lost and abandoned. They were so different from home. They even spoke different."

There is a noticeable difference between the accent in this area and other parts of the province. Like Dr. Alfred Doolittle, the discerning ear can identify which bay and even which part of the bay the speaker has lived. The Irish lilt of Deep Harbour emphasised the distance between their new home and their old. The girls were homesick, lonesome and almost despondent.

Alice Weller showed them through the house. It was a simple bungalow with three bedrooms along one side, kitchen and living room along the other, a bathroom at the far end and a porch at the entrance. The basement was open and unfinished with crushed stone for a floor and accessed through stairs in the porch.

The first bedroom was for the girls. It was adequate with two bunk beds. Next was their son David's room. He would soon be returning from high school. At the end of the hall was the master bedroom.

There, over the bed, Tammy saw a colour picture of the Virgin Mary holding in her arms the baby Jesus. The colours were loud and the whole thing was illuminated by an electric light at the top of the frame. Tammy liked it immediately.

But once again the two sisters reacted in opposite manners to their new home. For Maggie the religious pictures contrasted with the protestant home they had grown up in and left behind.

They had been baptised, confirmed and given their bibles in Deer Lake.

She remembered the Anglican Church where she and Tammy had sung in the choir. She remembered her family coming out to hear their two voices sweetly ringing through the church. Maggie knew they sang well and remembers how proudly the two of them basked in the approval of their foster parents and the congregation. The pride, love, family and everything she wanted was in that church in that moment. It was gone now far into the distant past.

She looked at the garish picture over the bed. She saw the mother tenderly holding her child with a sweetly sad look, perhaps mindful of the suffering the baby must undergo in his own life.

Maggie thought of her own mother when she was a child in St. John's, and she thought of Rita in Deer Lake. Tears fought their way to her eyes but she held them back.

Alice showed the girls the rest of their new home. The other side of the house comprised the kitchen-dining area and through an arch way the living room with the all-important television set.

Looking into the living room from the dining area Tammy could see the TV at the far wall on the left. At the other end, to her immediate right and almost out of sight behind the partition, was the armchair. On the arm of the chair she saw a hand, then an arm in a plaid shirt illuminated by the flickering, powder blue light from the television. In the armchair sat Albert Weller. He looked up from television and smiled a greeting to the girls. He seemed nice enough, Maggie thought.

Next to the TV, down the main wall was the chesterfield. Across from it was the large living room window. In the middle of the room was the coffee table.

Unlike Deer Lake, Tammy was liking this place more than Maggie was. She was now out of the tension and confusion of their departure from their last home.

Alice tactfully allowed the girls their privacy to unpack and adjust to the new surroundings. When her son David came home from school she brought the young man in for introductions. The sisters remarked that he was pleasant and friendly. But in spite of this it was a very sad night:

Tammy and I were very sad that first night. She may have blamed herself that we were there in the first place. We cried a lot. When Don Evans left we felt deserted. I tried to put a smile on my face whenever Alice came in the room. But I couldn't keep it there. I screeched and bawled. I didn't want to be there. I can still feel that atmosphere, how different it was from home.

On their first night at Wellers' foster home they sat on Tammy's lower bunk and cried in one another's arms. Maggie was broken hearted. The new home seemed like a foreign land.

Most of all Rita and Dick were no longer around. Prince, the Labrador Retriever, was far behind in her past. Tears convulsively pushed their way into Maggie's eyes and ran down her cheeks. She gave in to hysterical sobbing and would not leave her room. She was to remain there for days after her arrival in Deep Harbour, refusing to eat with the family.

All in all Tammy soon found Deep Harbour to her liking. She spent many of her days comforting the despondent Maggie. Tammy celebrated her fourteenth birthday in Deep Harbour two weeks after she arrived.

There were four Weller brother in their thirties and forties: Albert, Frank, Pat, and Levi. Their houses were built quite near one another.

A well-worn foot path connected two of the homes and Frank's barn in between them. Soon Tammy and Maggie were travelling those paths to visit Frank Weller's house. Frank's daughter Lisa became a close friend of Maggie. There was not a lot of contact with the Pat Weller family in the next house or the Levi Weller family in the fourth house on that hill.

All four Weller brothers were married and had children of their own. The father, Allan Weller, lived with Frank. They were, for the most part, likable fellows who generally got along with the community. They may have been a little clannish or secretive, but it was nothing that people found objectionable.

They were known as reliable workers and agreeable folks.

But this Weller family had a disease which affected many of the males, including Allan, Levi, Albert, Frank and Billy. The disease had survived for generations, protected and encouraged by the ogre of secrecy. Their disease is sexual abuse. In the majority of sexual abuse cases, the abuser is a generational victim himself.

Let us stop the clock and the calendar in this narrative at the fall of 1986 when Tammy first arrived. To try to understand what happened to her, let us go back in time to look at the sexual abuse practised and suffered by these men over the years. Let us look as well at the ogre of secrecy that concealed and protected it. *We can see that the key then as now is the silence of those who knew:*

Ann Wicks had left just four months before Tammy arrived in 1986. Ann had already confided to nurse Alicia Rollings that the reason for her leaving was the sexual abuse she had endured in the Albert Weller home. CF Camp coordinator Howse also knew of the abuse.

Two years before that, sixteen year old Dawn Williams had left after seven years of sexual abuse by Levi, son Billy and Albert Weller. She says she had revealed this abuse to a number of people including her boyfriend, several adult relatives of her natural family, and relatives of the foster family. As well, Dawn says she had informed at least two social workers of the sexual abuse by September of 1984.

In October of 1985, social worker Edith Decker had referred vaguely to Dawn's abuse by Levi Weller to the Director of Child Welfare, calling it an "implication", when in fact it was much more detailed and specific.

As well Edith had told the director of a report of a more heinous charge of alleged sexual abuse against Levi Weller. The alleged victim in this case had been a three year old child.

In 1985 there had been a report and an RCMP investigation of alleged sexual assault against a three year old girl. The parents reported that the child was sore and had told the mother that Levi Weller had inserted his finger into her vagina. Levi, a relative, had been babysitting the three year old at the time.

Levi denied all wrong doing and his lawyer sent the mother this letter on August 9, 1985:

> We have been retained by Mr. Levi Weller concerning allegations made by you that he has abused your three year old child. Mr. Weller informs me that this is not true and he is quite shocked and upset over these allegations.
>
> We have been informed that you are telling people of this alleged conduct, and we must inform you that this must stop immediately.
>
> We, therefore, demand that you cease and desist this slanderous behaviour and give our client a written apology. Our client has directed us to inform you that if no apology is forthcoming within ten (10) days from receipt of this letter then we have been asked to initiate action in District Court, which action will be based on slander and further our client has informed us that the whole matter may be turned over to Child Welfare for investigation.
>
> These are serious allegations and we must demand that you comply with this letter immediately.

Troubled by the lawyer's letter and resolved to protect their child, the mother and father visited the offices of the Department of Social Services, Child Welfare Division. There, on August 14th, 1985, they reported the alleged sexual abuse of their daughter by Levi Weller.

This was a year after Dawn Williams had accused Levi Weller of doing similar things to her from the time she had been nine until she was sixteen. The troubled parents may even have reported the alleged abuse against their daughter in the same office in St. John's that Dawn Williams reported hers.

With the three year old's parents involved, the allegation soon became a police investigation. The Baywood Detachment of the RCMP were to handle the investigation. On August 16, 1985, the commanding officer, Sgt. Norman Wood, assigned the investigation to Corporal Tom Barrett.

Sergeant Wood realized the practical problems of getting a conviction based on the evidence of an inarticulate three year old complainant. He noted to Barrett:

"Tom, if this offence did take place, the only way to prove it would be with a confession by the suspect because we are dealing with a three year old victim."

Levi Weller may have realized this simple fact as well, and he protested his innocence to the investigator. He referred to slander charges against his accusers. He even agreed to take a polygraph test to prove his innocence.

On September 3, 1985 Barrett interviewed the child with no success. He noted that a female officer may have better success, and the child was "reluctant to speak to me."

Sergeant Wood contacted the social worker for the area, Edith Decker. Edith advised him that one year previously, a girl named Dawn Williams had run away from Levi Weller's foster home. A mention had been made of sexual assault but it was felt that the girl was "just getting back" at her foster parents for the discipline they were trying to enforce. Edith told Sergeant Wood that there had been "nothing to it."

This was a year after Dawn had spoken clearly of her sexual assault to at least one social worker, even naming her tormentors, including Levi Weller.

On September 4, 1985 Corporal Barrett was transferred out of Baywood and Wood re-assigned the case to Constable Michael Dutois.

Dawn had also told her foster aunt about the sexual assault. The aunt was related to the three year old's mother. This may have been the manner in which the information reached the RCMP in Baywood that Levi had already been accused of sexually abusing another child in his care.

It may have been the "nothing to it" comment of Social Worker Edith Decker to Sergeant Wood that prompted an interview with Dawn. No reference was made to the detailed allegations of abuse that Dawn had already made to Social Services in St.John's. The RCMP and Edith Decker demonstrated no knowledge of this most vital information.

In any case Dawn was soon interviewed by Corporal B.A. MacLean of the RCMP in St. John's on September 18, 1985. Once again she told her story of abuse by Levi Weller. She explained that "she had been sexually assaulted in the foster-home from the time she was nine years old until she was thirteen or fourteen."

Once again it was recorded by officialdom and filed with the Baywood RCMP on September 30, 1985. Once again nothing was done about it. Instead of opening a separate file and investigation of Dawn's sexual abuse by Levi Weller, the RCMP saw her only as a supporting witness in the crime against the three year old. Again, nothing was done. The investigating officer filed it and the ogre of secrecy maintained control of the situation.

On November 14, 1985 Levi Weller gave a statement to yet another investigating officer, Constable Patricia Dutton of Baywood Detachment. In accord with departing investigator Bennet's recommendation a woman was handling the investigation dealing with alleged acts against the three year old.

Levi Weller appeared calm as he discussed the charges against him. He explained that the charges were false and that he was innocent of any wrong doing against the three year old or against Dawn. He offered to take a polygraph test to prove this and signed the polygraph consent form in the presence or the officer.

Constable Dutton sought other witnesses, such as the first foster child who had stayed briefly at the Levi Weller foster home. She arranged for Sergeant R.D. Russell to conduct the polygraph test on Levi Weller.

Dutton tried to contact Edith Decker, but told the Hughes Commission that it was difficult to do so as Edith was not returning her calls.

On November 6, 1985 Dutton reached Edith and arranged a meeting with the three year old, the parents and Edith. They used an anatomically correct doll but were unable to get much information from the child.

RCMP files indicate that Edith was not getting back to Dutois concerning the report on the interview with the three year old. The investigation was held up as the officers waited. Sergeant Wood wrote to his investigator: "Continue without her (Edith) if necessary."

Later at the Commission of Inquiry, Justice Hughes was perplexed by this difficulty of contact between the RCMP and the social worker, "The problem of getting in touch with the social workers recurs. RCMP should leave the message for the immediate return of all calls."

On December 9, 1985 Levi Weller was administered the polygraph test by Sergeant R.D. Russell of the RCMP. Russell observed that the subject was so agitated that he doubted a proper reading could be achieved. Dutton noted in her report that Weller "was very edgy and kept moving all the time."

Russell concluded that "there were irregularities in the polygram that prevented analysis." It is unclear why the polygraph was not re-administered. So, the final results were deemed inconclusive.

As Justice Hughes reports:

> Constable Dutton continued her investigation. On January 17, 1986 she re-interviewed the suspect who once again denied his involvement in any sexual offenses. Constable Dutton obtained a further statement from Ms. Williams on January 30 and reported 'I feel she is being truthful'. Constable Dutton testified before this commission that she was concentrating solely on trying to build a case around the allegation involving the three year old. Sergeant Wood was likewise concentrating on the child. In the file he noted to Constable Dutton:

'Patricia. All we have is Dawn Williams' evidence as you say. If you can get a similar story from the other foster child, we can have a look towards charges.'

The other child was never located. By this time she had grown to adulthood and moved to another province.

In April Dawn phoned Corporal MacLean who had interviewed her the previous September. She wanted to know how the investigation of Levi Weller had been proceeding. There was little he could tell her.

Constable Dutton submitted her final report to headquarters on May 12, 1986:

Due to the lack of evidence and the age of the child, it is felt there is nothing further that can be done in this matter. Based on the forgoing, this file will be concluded at this time.

Justice Hughes concluded that the officers had mishandled the investigation. He reflected critically on Dutton, Wood and the RCMP "reader" of the files in St. John's. All appeared before his commission.

Constable Dutton-Smith (as she now is) said she was very junior at the time and today she would handle the case differently. 'I definitely would have opened a separate file and viewed Ms. Williams' statement as a separate case.'

She said she focused solely on the case involving the three year old and never thought of proceeding with a charge against the suspect for sexually abusing Ms. Williams. She said that while she did have sufficient evidence to lay a charge in the Williams case, it just never occurred to her.

Sergeant Wood told Hughes that he now feels that the information provided by Dawn "should have been pursued as a separate matter.... It obviously slipped passed me."

As a result of poor investigation by the RCMP and poor communications by the Social Services Department, Tammy and Maggie King were placed in the Albert Weller foster home. From that point in time the tragedy was a ticking alarm clock wound tight and set for 6 p.m., August 7, 1988.

It is puzzling to realize that Edith Decker had not referred to Levi Weller's abuse of Dawn in her discussions with the RCMP. The allegation had been made by Dawn to the Social Services Department months before.

The incomplete RCMP investigation of Levi Weller had ended in the Spring of 1986. Ann Wicks had told nurse Rollings of abuse by Albert Weller in the summer of 1986. Dawn Williams had told the Social Services Department of abuse by Levi Weller and the alleged abuse by Billy Weller before the spring of 1986.

In spite of this level of reported abuse, no one was telling anyone about it. There was a polite silence about it in the community and among the officials who also knew. Absolutely nothing was done to protect the two girls, Tammy and Maggie King, age 13 and 12, who arrived in 1986. The ogre of secrecy had triumphed.

CHAPTER 8

LIFE IN DEEP HARBOUR

School days, school days,
Dear old golden rule days ...

Vaudeville, 1907, by Cobb & Edwards

The two King sisters went to school immediately that fall. On their first day at Appleton Junior High, they were met with dozens of scary ghosts, goblins and witches celebrating Halloween. The carnival atmosphere and the spooky costumes may have shocked them at first, but teachers and students made them feel welcome and the process of transition began. Tammy made friends in her new school where girls attended from the surrounding communities, including Deep Harbour. She developed lasting friendships with Sherri and Patsy Driscoll.

The girls spent many happy holidays with their Uncle Peter and their cousins in Mount Pearl. Maggie continued to do so but Tammy soon preferred to remain at the foster home on these occasions.

She was a good student who applied herself readily to her studies in spite of many distractions. A quiet girl, she was never a bother to her teachers and did little to call attention to herself. Her friends soon noticed a shy sense of humour that sometimes bubbled out of her almost against her wishes.

She was also an attractive girl, tall and well developed for her fourteen years. Soon Tammy was wearing very stylish and mature clothes. She took great pains and scrupulous care of her appearance as she had as a younger girl in Deer Lake.

At the Weller home, the girls quickly took to Alice, their foster mother. She was concerned about their welfare and offered herself as a confidant to them over the next two years.

"She was the mother I never had. Me and Tammy both could go to Alice and talk about anything, anything at all. She would give us her feelings on certain subjects, and that meant a lot to us."

This interview with Maggie took place at her sister Bonney's house. Maggie was now a young woman of 18 who was having some trouble in school and smoked Players Light cigarettes. She wore a light leather jacket with long fringes. She was lively and polite with an eagerness to answer my questions. She had a delicate beauty that combined vitality with frailty, like a young bird. Her long legs and good looks reminded me of Tammy.

"Did you talk to Alice about sexual subjects?"

"Yes, everything. I started my period there and I talked to Alice about it."

"Why didn't you tell her about the sexual activity with the men? Both of you were being sexually assaulted for two years and you did not confide in her. I cannot understand that."

She squirmed around trying to enlighten me about the situation they were living through. She then said, "I told her later. I told her about me and Frank."

"Did Tammy tell her about being sexually abused?"

"No. Not until the last day when Alice already knew."

"Why didn't she tell Alice?" Maggie's eye lids fluttered and she turned her slender body nervously in her chair and reached for a cigarette on the table.

"Maybe she couldn't."

The relationship between Tammy and Albert Weller appears, from the available evidence, to have begun shortly after the girls arrived in the fall of 1986. Tammy was then barely fourteen.

Maggie was in the living room one night when she heard a confusion of sounds coming from their bedroom. The Weller's son David was not at home and Alice was gone to bingo. She left the television and crept along the hall towards her bedroom where she peeped into the room.

Maggie recalled the scene, "The lights were on and Tammy was lying on the bottom bunk bed with her face to the wall. She was crying softly. Albert was kneeling beside her bed with one arm across her back. He was stroking or rubbing her back and comforting her."

"Don't worry, it'll be alright. Everything will work out fine," he said as he continued to rub her back.

Maggie described a confusion of emotions. First she was surprised at the level of intimacy between the two people in the room. She had no idea Albert and Tammy were so close. Maggie said later,

> Any other foster home we were in it was always the mother not the father who dealt with the children. It seemed unusual ... the feelings ... the mood in the room.

> I was so upset to see her crying.

> Tammy wasn't homesick. This wasn't ... this wasn't.... She was scared. I could tell ... Tammy was comforting me up till then. She wouldn't cry around me. She'd be the one I'd cry on. She'd comfort me.

> And then for me to look and see her crying and Albert with his arm around her. It didn't feel right cause Albert was a quiet man; he wasn't the one who would go in and talk to us.

> She didn't tell me about it! That's what was wrong. Something was going on that I did not know about and I wasn't told about ... I don't know ... all those feelings.

Another incident that first summer disturbed Maggie. Albert invited her and Tammy to go swimming with him.

We were delighted. It was like a special occasion for him to take us. He drove the truck in to the pond. There was no one else around except the three of us. He stayed on the shore and watched as we splashed around in the water.

It was cold and I was splashing Tammy and getting water in her hair. I was the tomboy. Tammy didn't want to get her hair mussed up.

Then Albert said: 'Maggie, you stop splashing Tammy.' We just ignored him and the next thing I knew he was very mad and shouting at me.

'Get out of the water. You hear me, Maggie! Get out of the water and go wait in the truck.' He was really upset.

I was confused and I started crying. I had to wait in the truck while Tammy stayed in the water and he stayed on the shore watching her. I can still see him watching her swimming by herself ...

There were times when I walked into the living room and the two of them were there alone. Albert would be sitting in his armchair leaning towards her on the chesterfield. She would be sitting right to the edge of the chesterfield beside him. When I walked in Albert would lean back quickly and Tammy would sit right still.

There were lots of opportunities for Tammy and Albert to be alone together. The Wellers had two dogs, a Boxer and a mutt.

Maggie said that it got to be a usual pattern for Tammy and Albert to walk the two dogs in the evenings. Two dogs and two leashes did not invite any more company and the two of them regularly walked through the quiet woods roads that surround the area. In this way they spent hours together in the wooded areas that surround their home.

In autumn the leaves of Deep Harbour turn red and gold in precious groves of deciduous amid a green sea of conifers. Little streams bounce and dance with clearings of dry grass and fallen hay.

There are trout in the ponds nearby and an occasional grouse will spring from the brush as you walk along the trails. Travellers have their favourite story of spotting a moose grazing in a clearing or bounding through the woods.

Cut-overs and burn-overs offer the walkers succulent feasts of ripe blue berries. The harvest, the bucolic beauty and the company tempts the travellers to pause and enjoy.

In summer the perambulators discover more delights, from languid and peaceful strolls in the heat of the day, to cool and refreshing hikes of an August evening. A swim in a nearby pond was often a perfect way to end a hot summer day. The fresh water ponds usually warmed up to briskly bearable by the end of a sunny day. The hardy found swimming to be a bracing sport, while the timid sat on the shore and watched. Tammy loved it and was an excellent swimmer. Albert often took her and Maggie, and often just Tammy to a secluded pond where she could swim undisturbed.

This pattern of time spent together soon became part of life for Tammy and Albert. They were getting to know each other in the course of enjoying long nature walks and late nights together watching television.

Eleven-year-old Maggie often complained that Tammy was Albert's favourite. Maggie often sensed that she was not entirely welcome with Tammy and Albert on their jaunts together.

Alice attended bingo many evenings and she often retired early. David and Maggie had school to attend week day mornings, so they usually were in bed early as well.

Tammy, however, had a different pattern of night time activity, as her sister Maggie pointed out.

Tammy was a real night owl. She was always the last one in the house to go to bed. She could go to bed late, like one or two in the morning and it'd be no problem for her to get up around seven o'clock the next morning.

It was always like that. So I'd leave the lamp on cause I never sleep with the light off. She'd always be the one to come in and turn off the light when she'd go to bed.

"Who else would be up in the nights?"

"Albert."

"Where were Alice and David?"

"They were in bed."

One day Maggie left to play with Lisa Weller at Frank's house. She knocked on the door and Frank answered it but instead of letting her in he put his arm around her and kissed her on the mouth. She pulled away but told no one of the incident.

Soon Frank was touching and kissing Maggie whenever he found her alone. He would hold her tightly in his arms and tell her how pretty she was.

"Was he affectionate?"

"Yes, I'd say he was. Now I was only a kid and he was a married man but it was kind of like on a date."

"A date?"

"Well, I was dating Johnny Wells at the time. You know how you are dating at twelve, holding hands and maybe a little kiss, stuff like that.

"Frank used to say, 'Kiss me like you kiss Johnny.' Or he would say, 'Does Johnny do this?' and he would touch me or make me touch him. But what he did to me Johnny and me never did."

"Did you tell Johnny?"

"No. Frank used to tell me about movies he liked to watch, dirty movies late at night when his wife wasn't around. He liked to watch the women. He used to tell me what they used to do in the movies. They used to take all their clothes off and stuff like that."

"Where would this occur?"

"At his house, in the kitchen or in the living room or sometimes we'd be up in his barn. He would take my hand an put it on him ...in places...."

"Where were Lisa and his wife when this was occurring?"

"They were always gone or in another room."

"You mean sometimes he would be touching you when someone was in the next room?"

"Yes. If someone came in he would just turn around right fast. He would be tense and I would be frightened. I knew it was wrong for him to do that because he was so ashamed of getting caught."

"How often did this occur?"

"Two or three times every week for almost two years."

"That was almost as long as you were there."

"Yes. He would kiss me and tell me I looked pretty. I was well developed for a twelve or thirteen year old. His hands would be all over me. I would be pulling away."

"How did you feel?"

"First I was surprised almost shocked. Then I was confused."

"Why were you confused?"

Long pause. "Guilty, maybe."

"Why would you feel guilty?"

"Because ... I felt something when he touched me. I was scared."

"Do you mean you were sexually aroused?"

"Yes, sometimes."

"It's complicated, isn't it."

"Very." Long pause. "This stuff that I'm telling you about ... no one else knows about it. Even Bonny doesn't know the extent ... It feels better after talking about it. I still feels at times like someone is watching me." She took a long draw on her cigarette.

"A man's form?"

"Yeah. Everywhere I turned when I was out there they were always there. Poppy or Albert or Frank." Here she screwed up her face in disgust. "They were always telling me and Tammy how beautiful we were, how our bodies were so mature for our ages, Cause, I mean when I was twelve I had the body of a fifteen year old. And Tammy certainly didn't look her age. She looked much older." She eagerly tried to explain the situation with the Wellers, as her voice went faster and her motions more animated.

"And they were always watching us with our shorts on or with a bathing suit on, telling us how beautiful we were. Their looks went right through me. Albert gave me those looks too, but that's all he did with me."

"Was Billy Weller ever there?"

"Not much that I recall."

"What about Levi Weller?"

"He had the same look in his eye as Albert and Frank whenever he came around."

"What about the other brother, Pat?"

She relaxed visibly. "Pat was a totally different story. I didn't see that look in his eyes. He was caring and sweet. The rest, you could tell by the look in their eyes what their intentions were."

"Did Frank threaten you in any way?"

"No. He told me not to tell Lisa, his daughter. We were close."

"Did you tell her?"

"No. Often he would give me some money when he was finished, like two dollars or something like that."

"A little bribe to keep you quiet?"

"Yeah, the same way with Poppy Weller."

"Did the old man touch you too?"

"Yes, lots of times."

"What would he do?"

"He'd grab me in his arms and kiss me. Once he tried to take off my clothes, but I got away. Poppy Weller was a big man and he would squeeze me real tight. He'd always say, 'Don't you tell Lisa'."

"Do you think they were doing anything bad with Lisa?"

A troubled shadow of a look went across her face. "I was really scared of that towards the end."

"Did you ever discuss it with her?"

"It's not an easy thing to talk about." She looked to her cigarette.

"So you have no evidence or reason to believe that they did anything to Lisa, right?"

No answer. So I continued the interview after checking my tape recorder.

"Would this be in the middle of the day?"

"Yes, sometimes in the morning. Poppy'd be wearing green workpants with a belt at the waist, and the same plaid shirt that they all wore."

"So tell me about this business of passing a two dollar bill or a five dollar bill by Frank or Poppy."

"I can't remember the number of times but every time you passed by them there was an incident."

"An incident?"

"Between Albert's house and Frank's house was Frank's barn. There was bushes all around it like trees and it was secluded from both houses' view. And you'd be walking across that area and they'd grab you and pull you in or ..."

"And sometimes they'd give you money?"

"Yes, I'd be on the way to the store or just up to Lisa's.

"They'd say, 'Come here I want you,' or they'd probably reach out and grab you and he'd have a great laugh at it because you were probably startled for a minute, or something like that. It was more playing around with you than physical force. An easy catch!"

"Do you think that Tammy was in love with Albert Weller?"

Here Maggie stubbed out her cigarette. Her answer came after some thought:

> She thought that she was. She a young
> girl who had never been with a man before.
> All of a sudden this man is so caring and so ...
> he's there for you. That can give you the
> signals.... She thought she was in love ...

I couldn't help notice how she changed from the pronoun "she" to the pronoun "you" as she described the relationship.

Her earnest tone was seeking to help me understand, and she was struggling for the right words. Her slender fingers waved in the air like birds.

"Tell me about some other people you and Tammy knew in Deep Harbour."

She relaxed in her chair at the kitchen table and took her coffee cup in her hands. "We used to visit John and Meigan Driscoll and their family. I used to buddy around with their children my own age. They were like the family I never had. They were always good to me and Tammy. We could always go there and feel safe."

"Another family we used to visit a lot was Francis and Loretta Driscoll, Sherri's and Dotti's mother and father. We used to spend a lot of time there. They were nice people."

" How did you get along with David Weller?"

She smiled again. "He was really nice. He was a real brother and a good friend to Tammy especially. They used to go in the room and plan their weekend together. They hung around together but there was nothing sexual. It was like a real brother and sister relationship. David used to carry on and joke around all the time."

"Tell me about Alice Weller."

"She was a good mother to us. We had many open chats and we could talk about anything with her."

"Did you say you told her about Frank assaulting you?"

"Not right away, but I did eventually tell Alice. Little by little I asked her about sexual abuse, what it was and stuff like that. Then one day I told her about what Frank was doing with me. I was crying. She talked it over with me." Maggie reached for another cigarette.

"Did she report it to the police or to the Department of Social Services?"

"No. She told Albert. He said that he would talk to Frank about it. She told him to make sure Frank stayed away from me."

"Did Frank stay away from you after that?"

"No. As far as I know Albert never told him."

"Why didn't you tell other people, like the police or the social workers?"

"We didn't want any trouble and we didn't want to be sent to a group home."

"What was a group home supposed to be like?"

"It was horrible. No one cared about you and no one wanted you in a group home. You were practically treated like dirt in a group home." She shivered slightly in her chair and wrapped her arms around herself. "No one cared about you, and me and Tammy knew that we were better than that."

"Would you have gone to a group home?"

"No. Me and Tammy had talked about it many times. We had decided to make away with ourselves if we had to go into a group home. Alice knew about it." She reached for the cigarette in the ashtray.

"How were you planning to make away with yourselves?"

"We never discussed the details but we had an agreement between me and Tammy that if they tried to move us we were going to make away with ourselves."

"Kind of a suicide pact?"

"That's right." She bit her lower lip grimly.

"Did you and Tammy always get along well? Were you close?"

"We were close, but we didn't always get along very well."

"What do you mean?"

"She was always so fussy over herself, always doing her hair and looking in the mirror, and sometimes we'd fight over clothes."

"How so?"

"Well, we'd be sarcastic to each other. First we used to fight about if we should go back to Deer Lake or stay with the Wellers. I always wanted to go back to Deer Lake.

"I used to get spitey and sometimes I'd say 'I hate you.' But she always would answer, 'Well, I don't hate you.' I feel so bad about it now."

"Why didn't you tell the social workers about the sexual abuse? They were there to protect you."

"They're another story!" She looked away in disgust.

During the periods of these abuses the four girls were under the care and control of the Director of Child Welfare.

Maggie reflected on the role of the Social Services Department in her life. Her comments centred around the most puzzling dimension of this whole sordid affair: Why did the girls not reveal the abuse to the social workers who visited the home on a regular basis? I asked Maggie and she quickly answered:

"We didn't get to see them often enough to trust them. You can't tell that kind of thing to a stranger."

Maggie's and Tammy's sister Bonny, who spent most of her life in the foster care system, said the same thing:

> The social workers come and go. It could be a new one almost every time. If you confide to them that you are being physically or sexually abused in your foster home, they go back to their office and file a report. You have got to stay in the home and live with your abusers.

> You can be taken out of that home and put God knows where, perhaps in a worse situation. When you complain, you lose all control of the situation. The system takes over.

"Maggie, what did you think of your social workers?"

"We had two main ones, Edith Decker and Madonna Hynes. Madonna Hynes seemed like a nice lady."

"Did you or Tammy mention the problem of sexual assault to the social workers?"

"No."

"Why not?"

"They were strangers." She became cool and adamant. "How could you trust them? There was never any privacy. They'd come in and we'd all sit down at the kitchen table. There'd be me and Tammy and Alice and sometimes Albert and the social worker. We never had a chance to talk to them privately until after." She was stubbing out the butt.

"After what?"

She didn't even look up but answered almost dreamily. "After the RCMP were called and everything fell apart."

CHAPTER 9

THE ABUSE IS EXPOSED

Things fall apart; the centres cannot hold;
Mere anarchy is loosed upon the world,
The blood-dimmed tide is loosed, and everywhere
The ceremony of innocence is drowned;
The best lack all conviction, while the worst
Are full of passionate intensity.
Surely some revelation is at hand.

W.B. Yeats, "The Second Coming"

In spite of all the prior revelations of sexual abuse by Dawn Williams and Ann Wicks, to social workers, aunts, boyfriends, foster brothers, RCMP officers and others, the lid never did come off the Weller foster home until a most innocuous event in July of 1988. The ogre of secrecy had sat on his family treasure for years and perhaps for generations. Silence was maintained by all.

The ogre was toppled from his seat by a serendipitous conversation between a social worker at the Janeway Children's Hospital named Cindy Wilbur, and nurse Alicia Rollings. Rollings casually inquired how Ann Wicks was dealing with her many problems including the sexual assaults in her former foster home.

It had been two years since Ann had confided in Rollings and Rollings had revealed it to C.F. Camp Coordinator, Ruth Howse. She had assumed that the coordinator had discussed it with others, including social worker Cindy Wilbur.

Wilbur, formerly from New World Island, had known Ann Wicks since about 1981 through her work at the Janeway. Wilbur told a surprised Nurse Rollings that she was hearing about the sexual assaults for the first time.

Cindy Wilbur changed everything in this story. She did not maintain the polite silence. Unlike all others who knew about Ann's abuse up to that date, Cindy Wilbur complied with Section 49 of the Child Welfare Act of Newfoundland which requires anyone knowing of an alleged child abuse to report it to the Director of Child Welfare. Neglect to do so was, and still is, punishable by law. The date is a most important one in this narrative:

TUESDAY, JULY 19, 1988

On Tuesday, July 19, 1988, Cynthia Wilbur contacted the Department of Social Services Offices in Shipley, which was responsible for the area of Deep Harbour. Her eventful telephone conversation with the Shipley offices made clear the extent of the alleged abuse and the names of the abuser and the victim. At last the abuse was formally reported by someone in authority to someone in authority. The incidents were on the official record, documented; professional people were now on task. Wheels should have started turning because there were six weeks left before a desperate Tammy would run to her last escape route. As the Hughes Royal Commission states:

"The foster home was identified and it was immediately known that the King sisters, both foster-children, were then living in that same foster home."

Wilbur named Ann Wicks as the alleged victim and Albert Weller as the alleged perpetrator. The two social workers responsible for that area were Edith Decker and Madonna Hynes. Edith was on educational leave at the time until August 10, so Madonna Hynes started the investigation for the Social Services Department. In fact the phone call from Cynthia Wilbur was received by Sandra Witherall, a summer student worker at the Shipley office.

According to Highes Commission files, Madonna Hynes did not contact the RCMP for another ten days, until July 29, 1988.

She did contact Karen Khan, Social Work Program Coordinator for the Child Welfare Division, on the next day, Wednesday, July 20, 1988. The decision of that conversation was to have Ann interviewed in Catalina by a social worker in that area. Hynes told this to Cynthia Wilbur, who had made the initial complaint, and Wilbur spoke against the idea. She felt that Ann was not in a stable home environment and would not receive the support she needed to report and follow through in court. Ann's supposed threats of suicide were also a concern.

It was therefore decided to have Alicia Rollings arrange to have Ann interviewed at the Janeway Hospital with "key support personnel present."

Karen Khan, Madonna Hynes and now Sandra Witherall discussed what to do. They felt that they did not have enough information to confront Albert Weller. They did not contact the RCMP and reveal what they did know.

They decided to go out to Deep Harbour the next day and interview Tammy outside the foster home. They contacted her at the Deep Harbour town council office where she worked as a summer student.

Madonna Hynes did not know Tammy, so Sandra Witherall came along. Sandra had completed the child progress report on Tammy and Maggie on May, 25, 1988. Unlike Madonna, she had actually met the girl. It was agreed that this familiarity would be essential if Tammy was to talk freely about her foster home situation.

"It was once again realized that we know so little about our foster children and we needed to establish an ongoing relationship whereby if there was anything to talk about, the girls would feel comfortable in that they were not talking to strangers."

These comments from the Social Work Coordinator for Child Welfare, Karen Khan, seem at this point to be a somewhat obvious observation.

THURSDAY, JULY 21, 1988

So, on Thursday, July 21, 1988, Hynes and Witherall interviewed Tammy at the Deep Harbour town hall. Tammy appeared relaxed and forthright. She was an attractive fifteen year old who sat poised if not completely relaxed before the two social workers. Witherall began as soon as they were alone in the town council office:

"Tammy, this is Madonna Hynes, my boss. She is a social worker in Shipley."

"Hi Tammy, how are you?" Madonna was easy to warm to.

"I'm fine." Tammy still sat erect in her clean jeans and sneakers with her legs crossed and her hand joined on top of them.

"Tammy we want to ask you a few questions as part of our regular child progress report. Is that OK?"

"Yes. That's fine."

"How are things going in your foster home?"

"Things are going fine."

"How do you get along with Alice Weller?"

"Just fine. She is excellent."

"How do you get along with Albert Weller? Any problems there?"

"No problems at all. We get along fine."

"What about David?"

"We get along great; he's fun to be with."

Questions were asked concerning household activities, outings in an attempt to determine patterns of behaviour.

"If you had a problem is there someone you would be able to talk to?"

"I could talk to both Albert and Alice if I had a problem. But I don't."

In her report of the interview, Karen Khan wrote that Tammy:

> ... was relaxed and didn't appear tense. Any initial uncomfortableness could be related to the fact that this was 'new' to her. She was not used to sitting down and discussing issues with a social worker. It is not an established process or procedure due to the high caseloads.

That comment indicates a foster care system in which these children float about under little actual observation or evaluation by those charged with their care.

In short, Tammy indicated that everything was fine. She described her foster home as 'the best', and gave a very positive picture of her life with the Wellers.

On their way back the two social workers dropped in to the Albert Weller house but no one was at home.

FRIDAY, JULY 22, 1988

The next morning, Friday, July 22, 1988, Hynes received a telephone call from an irritated Alice Weller.

"Can you tell me why the interview was done outside the home? Usually they are done here at the house?"

"Yes, we dropped by your house later but there was no one at home."

"I can't help but wonder what's up? It seems strange that we were left out of the interview."

"No, we are just trying to get to know our foster children and get an understanding of how they are doing in foster care. That's all."

"Have you had a complaint against our foster home?"

"No, nothing like that."

"If you got a complaint against this foster home, then I will turn in my licence."

The second last weekend in July came and went with the tension in the Albert Weller household turned up just one more of many successive notches.

On Monday, July 25, 1988, Sandra Witherall called the Janeway Children's Hospital to discover that Ann was still unable to come for an interview with Social Services personnel. It took until Thursday to arrange the interview.

THURSDAY, JULY 28, 1988

On Thursday, July 28, Ann was brought in from Catalina to the Janeway Hospital where she met with the social workers in Cindy Wilbur's office. Present were Madonna Hynes, Cindy

Wilbur and Alicia Rollings, the nurse to whom Ann had first disclosed the abuse two years before.

Ann was now 21 years old. She sat in the chair transfixed with horror at the prospect of revealing the abuse. The ordeal of telling others terrified the girl more than the fear of the actual abuse. She was a study in the code of silence that surrounds these offences.

"I don't want to go through with it. I can't tell it to the police."

"You don't have to if you don't want to."

"It's so embarrassing. He made me ..." Ann dissolved into shuddering sobs.

"You don't have to go to the police, but you should tell us what happened there."

"There are other girls in the home and they may be in danger of the same thing. Please tell us what happened," Madonna asked Ann simply.

"OK, I'll tell you, but I won't make any statement to the police. If charges are laid I'll have to go to court."

"Why don't you want to go to court?"

"Everyone will blame me and not him. My father will blame me and my family will be hurt."

"We won't blame you. Tell us what Albert Weller did to you."

Ann began with great emotion, to tell her story of countless sexual assaults by Albert Weller starting soon after she arrived at the home on March 24, 1983. She described how Albert avoided detection by Alice and how much of the abuse occurred on "Bingo Nights."

It was a sad tale of confusion and grief which the distraught young woman relayed to her listeners. It was a difficult and emotional interview.

When Madonna got back to her office later that same day she contacted Karen Khan at regional office. They decided to contact the RCMP in Baywood, which was the nearest detachment to the Deep Harbour foster home.

Then Karen Khan contacted a lawyer at the Department of Justice, Cathy Crocker. The latter informed Khan that they must be concerned about "the protection of the children currently in the home."

It was becoming apparent that they or the RCMP were going to have to confront the Wellers with the allegations. Karen Khan had doubts in the reliability of the complainant, Ann Wicks, whom she later told Justice Hughes "had a history of being unstable."

FRIDAY, JULY 29, 1988

Madonna Hynes "recalls" contacting the RCMP in Baywood on Thursday, July 28, 1988, on the same day as Ann's interview. She cannot recollect the name of the officer she spoke with. She said that the unnamed officer was supposed to get back to her.

RCMP records, on the other hand, indicate that Madonna first called at 3 p.m. on Friday July 29, 1988. The Hughes Inquiry also recorded July 29 as the date of the first call to the RCMP from Social Services. The RCMP Data Entry Sheet for that day recounts:

> Madonna Hynes of Social Services reported a 20 year old female resident now living in Catalina was sexually assaulted 2-3 years ago at a foster home in Deep Harbour. Requests assistance.

The Continuation Report that followed was dated the same day and was signed by Officer Newbury and Investigating Officer Camville. It lamented that the original allegation to the nurse two years before had not been reported. It noted as well that The Department of

> ... Social Services are going to start an investigation as there are other girls still in this foster home. The victim is adamant that she doesn't wish this to be a police matter or to go court with same. Hynes wishes to know if the RCMP can come to see the victim at the Social Services office to explain to her the judicial system and any protection that is available to her.

The RCMP were going into this situation with several serious handicaps: The girl was refusing to lay charges and Social Services would not reveal the name of the alleged perpetrator. They did not even know which foster home was involved. The Mounties knew they needed to interview the girl.

The investigating officer, Camville, was also under the misapprehension that Social Services could not "approach the home to see if other sexual assaults have taken place," unless the unknown girl made a complaint.

Camville tried to phone Hynes at 4 p.m. that same day, July 29, 1988, but there was no answer.

His commanding officer, Corporal Newbury, wrote in the continuation report that same evening:

> The social worker or any other adult person is required to report when victim is a child. The victim in this is no longer a child although the alleged offenses happened when she was 16-18 years of age. I don't know off hand if the social worker is still compellable.

They were obviously considering forcing Madonna to reveal the names of the principals involved.

MONDAY, AUGUST 1, 1988

On Monday, August 1, 1988, a new investigating officer was charged with the case. Corporal Newbury wrote a note to the new investigating officer, Constable Ronald Green, who had just been handed the file. The note said simply: "Contact S.S. and see if you can get to the bottom of this."

Ronald Wayne Green was born in 1952 in British Columbia. On entering the force, his training was the standard six month course offered by the RCMP to new recruits.

Following his graduation from the RCMP training course, he was stationed mainly in Alberta from 1981 to 1985. He later told Justice Hughes that his duties during this time included enforcing the migratory game bird regulations, transporting prisoners, customs and excise, and immigration and passport.

From 1985 to 1988 he was stationed at the three man RCMP detachment in Bow River, Alberta.

In mid July of 1988 he was transferred to the eight man Baywood detachment in Newfoundland. Sergeant Don Hilton had recently been taken command of the detachment.

Green had completed no psychology courses or other specific training in sexual offences. He had little experience to investigate a sexual assault allegation. In fact, this was the first sexual assault investigation that he had headed. He told Hughes that he had handled "a few" such cases, but only as an "assistance" to another officer who was heading the case.

Green was a central figure in this unfortunate chronicle. He soon demonstrated a procrastination that followed him through the investigation. He had the file for over a week before he made an entry in the Continuation Report. On August 8, Green recorded that he had made one phone call: "August 8, 1988: Called Soc. Ser. 834-2015. Hynes on another line. Message left for her to call back."

The next day his entry in the Continuation Report reads as follows: "August 9, 1988: Called again to Soc. Ser. Hynes out. Will call back on the 10th."

But the Social Services Department had already started their own investigation. Hynes and Karen Khan discussed the situation. They were frustrated by Ann's refusal to give a statement to the RCMP. They decided that their only recourse was to go out to Deep Harbour and confront Albert Weller and his wife with the allegations. They would observe the reaction and see how the Wellers reacted. Perhaps there would be a confession or an explanation. Madonna phoned Alice Weller and set up an appointment for August 2nd, Albert's next day off.

TUESDAY, AUGUST 2, 1988

On Tuesday, August 2, 1988, Madonna Hynes and summer student Sandra Witherall drove out to Deep Harbour to visit the Weller foster home. Albert and Alice were there and Tammy was in her bedroom, probably listening closely to the conversation.

Seated at the Weller's kitchen table Madonna Hynes soon came to the point:

"We have an allegation of sexual abuse against Mr. Weller, and we have to investigate it."

Both Albert and Alice Weller appeared shocked by the sudden revelation.

"Who would say such a thing?" Alice asked.

"We cannot reveal the identity of the alleged victim at this time."

"I didn't abuse anyone." Albert protested.

"This is a horrible slander and we'll get a lawyer to sue whoever made up such a lie."

This is reminiscent of the letter from Levi Weller's lawyer to the three-year-old's parents exactly three years before.

"Can't the courts force such a person to come forward and account for these accusations?" Alice asked.

"I don't know," Madonna answered.

"I've worked with Provincial Parks for twenty years and I have never had a complaint like this before. This could affect my job."

"And our good names in the community. If this gets around, that Albert is sexually abusing his foster children...." She paused to contemplate the horrible thought.

"I am not sure if you understand the serious legal implications of this charge. I know that it is an embarrassment in the community but it is also a serious criminal offence punishable by a jail term."

"I'd just like to know who would make up such a story," Albert said.

"How can we defend our good name when we don't even know who is making the charges?" Alice was frustrated by the injustice of it all.

"Could we interview the girls?" Madonna asked.

"Of course. Tammy is in her room and Maggie should be back soon."

"Could we do it privately?"

"Yes. Why don't you go in her bedroom and talk to her there?"

That is what Madonna did.

"Hi Tammy, can I come in?"

"Sure."

Tammy was sitting on the bottom of two bunk beds with a doodle pad on her lap. The writing pad was small, diary size, about one quarter of the size of a normal sheet of writing paper.

"What are you writing?"

"Oh, nothing." Tammy laid it aside and gave her attention to the social worker.

"Tammy, I have something very serious to talk to you about. There has been an accusation made against Mr. Weller."

"What is it?"

"Someone has said that he sexually assaulted a girl who was staying here."

"What?"

"Do you understand what I mean by sexual assault?"

"Yes, I think so."

"It means that he was touching her in private places on her body."

"Yes, I know what you mean."

"Has he ever done anything like that to you?"

"No, of course not. That's ridiculous."

Madonna could see Tammy become angry. "What kind of a person would make that kind of a charge against Albert? He's so kind he wouldn't hurt a fly."

"Do you feel comfortable around him?"

"Yes, I feel perfectly comfortable around him," Tammy said clearly.

"How do you feel about Alice?"

"I love her like a mother. She is always good to us."

"Do you get along well with David?"

"He is a perfect brother to us. We get along great."

Madonna could see that Tammy was getting upset. Suddenly the girl asked, "Does this mean we'll be moved out of here?"

"No, I didn't say that."

"I'm happier here than I have ever been. I don't want to move away from here. It's so unfair."

Around 5 p.m. that evening, Madonna Hynes interviewed Tammy's sister, Maggie. As the Social Services report prepared by Karen Khan states:

165

Maggie confirmed with Ms. Hynes what Tammy had already stated. She was very angry that someone could say such a thing and seemed to be genuinely surprised that we were inquiring about Albert Weller's behaviour towards her. She said Albert is really nice and both her and Tammy love living with them.

She said she is able to talk to both of them and they all laugh and joke a lot. She said Alice often talks to both of them about making sure to let her know if something happens that is inappropriate such as someone making advances towards them. So she said that she would definitely know if Albert had even tried anything with her. Her concern was also about what was going to happen to them and she also stated that she did not want to leave the Weller home.

Tammy and Maggie were so upset with the social workers that Alice had to calm the girls and encourage them to continue to talk with Hynes. "She's got to ask these questions; she's only doing her job," Alice said to the two troubled girls.

Tammy looked at Madonna Hynes, "If you move us out of here we'll only run away and come back. This is the best home we ever had."

"Yes we will," her sister, Maggie chimed in.

Then, according to the final report written by Karen Khan, Hynes and Witherall sat down at the kitchen table with Alice and the two girls. Before leaving the house the five women discussed sexual assault risks to the girls and protection concerns of the Department of Social Services.

The girls assured Hynes that there was nothing happening and if anything did occur they would immediately report it to her. Alice assured the social workers that she was well able to protect the girls from any dangers of this kind, if there were any dangers.

Alice did not mention to Social Worker, Hynes, that Maggie had been sexually assaulted by Albert's brother, Frank Weller.

The next day was Wednesday, August 3, 1988. Karen Khan at Regional Office and Madonna Hynes consulted once more, trying to decide what to do. They still lacked an accuser who would come forward. The two sisters seemed fine and both had protested that nothing bad was happening. In fact they had clearly stated that they loved the Weller foster home.

The social workers decided to leave the two girls in the home until an investigation showed some evidence to support Ann Wick's charge.

Monday, August 8, 1988. Madonna Hynes got a phone call from Alice Weller, who was agonizing over the allegations against her husband. She wondered if there was some way to resolve the matter. Madonna promised to let her know of any developments.

WEDNESDAY, AUGUST 10, 1988

On August 10 Constable Green finally got hold of Madonna Hynes. It was now twelve days since Hynes had reported the accusation to the RCMP in Baywood, and nine days since Green had been given the file.

Madonna had much to tell Constable Green once contact was finally made between them. She gave Ann Wick's name and age as 21. She told Green that the alleged abuser was Albert Weller of Deep Harbour. Ann had been 15 and 16 during the years of the abuse, which had begun with fondling and touching and eventually progressing to intercourse.

Hynes further advised Green that Ann was very immature for her age. Mention may also have been made of Ann's debilitating physical disease.

"Have you interviewed Albert Weller?" Green asked.

"We interviewed both Albert and his wife. He denies sexually assaulting anyone. He wanted to know who made the allegations."

"Did you inform him?"

"No. Ann is not sure what she is going to do."

"Might she testify in court?"

"No, she is adamant that she doesn't want the police involved. But there is something else."

"Yes?"

"There are two teenage girls still living in the foster home." Madonna waited for the significance of this statement to sink in.

"Is Albert Weller still living there too?" Green asked.

"Yes he is."

Green was silent at the end of the line as he considered the implications of what he had just heard.

Hynes quickly added, "I spoke to both girls, they seem happy and well adjusted. They were both interviewed individually and both denied anything has happened to them. In fact they seemed to resent the suggestion of any wrongdoing by their foster father."

"Did they seem to be forced or threatened into silence?"

"No, they seem to be quite outspoken. I am sure that one of them would speak out if anything was wrong."

"What's the Wicks girl's problem? Why won't she come forward with a statement?" Green inquired.

"It's the embarrassment. Her family in Catalina doesn't know about it and she doesn't want them to find out."

Their phone conversation ended with this information being exchanged. Green's commanding officer, Dutois, read and signed the Continuation Report the following week.

FRIDAY, AUGUST 12, 1988

On August 12, 1988 Madonna Hynes noted in a letter to the Director of Child Welfare, Frank Simms, that "... the Wellers now have a female sibling group in their foster home, Tammy King age 15 and Maggie King, age 13 years."

As well, Karen Khan passed on information to her superiors on a continuing basis. Ann was now living in Catalina with her "possessive and over-protective" natural father. Both Cindy Wilbur and Alicia Rollings were in regular contact with Ann. They were concerned about what Karen Khan called Ann's "... mental ability to handle this. They felt she was suicidal and did talk of killing herself before. They said she was already under a lot of stress ..."

On Friday, August 12, 1988, Social worker Edith Decker

visited the Weller foster home. Just two days back from education leave, she was there to familiarize herself with the situation.

Alice was home alone and the two women discussed the alleged assaults.

"I'm trying to figure who in Deep Harbour would make such a charge against this home," Alice said.

"We have to investigate these charges; there may be some truth to them and the girls may be in danger." Edith was the regular social worker for the Weller foster home.

"If I thought that Albert was doing that I would get a gun and blow his brains out. I know where there is a gun and I would do it."

Tammy then came home and sat at the table with them. Discussion freely continued about the allegations and once again Tammy told a social worker that she could not believe that this had been said about Albert Weller. Once again Tammy denied all wrong doing by Albert Weller. The social workers were in an awkward spot.

TUESDAY, AUGUST 16, 1988

The Baywood RCMP Continuation Report entry for August 16, 1988 is neatly typed and signed by the new commanding officer, Sergeant Don Hilton. The musical chairs of RCMP investigators and commanders had once again changed in the Baywood detachment. Constable Ron Green, remained as chief investigating officer.

On August 16, 1988, Sergeant Hilton wrote:

> Ron:
>
> Edith Decker of Social Services called. Apparently Ann Wicks had decided to go see Alice Weller about this and they have not been able to talk her out of it.
>
> In view of this I suggested they try to have her come see us first and if this fails to at least accompany Ann and have the meeting

with Alice somewhere Mr. Weller will not
walk in on them.

Please arrange to see the victim as soon
as you can.

Thanks,
Don Hilton

Ann Wicks was determined to talk to Alice before she would
make any statements. Her love for Alice Weller and reluctance to
hurt her former foster mother may have been part of Ann's
refusal to report to the RCMP.

The ever resourceful Cindy Wilbur once again prevailed and
convinced Ann not to see Alice Weller before testifying to the
RCMP.

On the same day, August 16, Hilton again wrote:

Decker called back. **Ann Wicks has**
agreed to talk to us and has decided not to talk
to Alice Weller. Decker would like to have her
talked to as soon as possible. I advised her
you would make an effort to see her in the
next day or so. The meeting can be arranged
through Decker if you want to go this route ...

Also on August 16, a concerned Officer Michael Dutois
writes in the Continuation Report:

Ron: are we waiting to hear back from
Social Services or what? I feel Albert should
be spoken to regardless of what Social
Services say, check with Doug, I think he
would say the same. We have an allegation.

The last word was underlined twice. There is a tone of
impatience and insistence in the message. It should be noted that
Officer Michael Dutois had been the investigator in the alleged
sexual assault of Levi Weller against the three year old back in

1985. Dutois was still in Baywood and his memory of that earlier case may have prompted his insistence in this later investigation of Levi's brother, Albert Weller.

Before the Hughes Inquiry, Dutois explained that he felt that Albert Weller should have been questioned. He felt that Weller could have been summoned and charged then. This would make sense, for now the RCMP had the names of the alleged victim and perpetrator as well as willingness on Ann's part to testify. Coupled with the knowledge that two girls were still in the home, it is a pity Dutois's direction was not followed.

Ron Green made another phone call to Social Services. This time he spoke to Edith Decker who was now handling the case at the Shipley Social Services Office. Ann Wicks was finally ready to talk to the police. Arrangements were made to interview Ann the next day in Shipley. It was to be a landmark day in the investigation, for Ann, when she finally spoke, had a lot to say.

WEDNESDAY, AUGUST 17, 1988

Cindy Wilbur accompanied Ann Wicks to the fateful interview with RCMP officer Ron Green on August 17, 1988. It took place at the Shipley Social Services offices and Edith Decker was also present.

In the tragic sequence of events, this is a very significant date. From August 17 onwards, the investigating officer had a detailed statement of offences, with the name and address of the alleged perpetrator. This is the most important date in the chronology of this case. Any legitimate official hesitation to react should now have disappeared.

The interview lasted from 4 p.m. to 7 p.m. It was agonizing for all concerned, especially for Ann Wicks. She broke down and cried often. She found the sexual vocabulary which she had to use to communicate her assaults awkward and embarrassing. It was difficult for her to even say many of the words.

Ann also agonized over what would happen now that she had made the revelations. Even as she sat in front of Constable Green to tell her story, Ann was still locked in a mortal struggle with the ogre of secrecy. She had the strength to win that painful struggle.

Green wrote down what Ann painfully said and then read it

back to her. She and the others all signed and dated the document. Sensitive readers be warned that this passage contains several graphic sexual references.

Ann Wicks, born July 31, 1967, age 21

I am presently living in Catalina with my father Ronald Wicks. I have been there since the summer of 1986. I moved to his house from the Albert Weller residence in Deep Harbour. I had lived at Weller's since the 24th of March 1983. I was 15 years old - due to turn 16 in July of 1983. All was fine during 1983. I stayed in my own bedroom. There was Albert, his wife Alice, and their son David. He is 1 year younger than me.

In early 1984 Albert started to make passes at me. He started out by grabbing at my behind as he passed. He'd grab and squeeze. He didn't say anything about it that I recall. He used to do it to Alice as well. I didn't think it was so wrong. I felt that was just his way. I would tell him to stop but I didn't get mad at him either. This went on for several weeks.

He went in steps from then on. He would drink beer during the evening. He would take beer bottle caps and put them down my top. He would pull my shirt out and drop the cap in. He would laugh at it. He wasn't putting his hand in my shirt or saying anything about what he was doing. He could drink a half dozen beer during the course of a night without getting drunk. He went on from this to touching my breast outside my clothing. He would also make motions to touch my crotch area but I would avoid it.

It happened numerous times. Sometimes when I was going by, sometimes when I was just standing he'd come up to me. He touched with his fingers, pinched lightly, or used his whole hand.I didn't like it so I tried to avoid being where he could do it. I would tell him to stop it and leave me alone. Nobody ever heard because he would do it when there was no one around. Alice would be out somewhere and David would be at a friends.

Albert went from this to on numerous times taking my hand -usually the right hand - because I sat on the chesterfield and he sat on a chair beside it - and he would put it on his pants in his crotch area.

He would tell me to feel it to see what would happen to it. His penis was hard. I would try to pull my hand away but he would hold my wrist. He would let me struggle a little while before he would let me go. He used to tell me not to tell anyone about what was happening.

I was scared. I didn't want Alice to know what he was doing because I knew it would hurt her. These things would happen when Alice was either out or in bed. She would sometimes take a nap after supper, or go to bed. She would go to bed about 11 p.m. He wouldn't do it all the time, I never knew when, though.

Sometimes David would watch TV with us. Nothing ever happened while he was there. He did it usually about 3 or 4 times a week. This was during 1984.

Albert went from this to touching me inside my clothes. It would usually happen in the evening when we were watching TV and Alice and David were always out when he did it. He would lean over from his chair toward me. In order for me to watch TV I would sort of lay on my side with the top of my head towards Albert and my feet towards the other end of the chesterfield.

He would put his hand inside my shirt. I always wear a brassiere. He would put his hand inside my brassiere. He never said anything other than to try and convince me to let him go on. I would cross my hands over my chest and sometimes try to pull his hand away. I would tell him not to do it. He didn't hold on to me or put his other arm around me during these times. He would also get out of his chair and either kneel in front of me or stand in front of me.

When he was in front of me he would put his hand or hands up from the bottom of my shirt. I always wore T-shirts. He would pull my brassiere up and touch my breasts. I was scared to cause a commotion for Alice to hear so sometimes he would stay for a while.

He tried sometimes to kiss me on the lips. I would turn my head away. He would try to pull my T-shirt up too. Sometimes he would get it up over my breasts. I would try to pull it down but he would also be trying to undo my pants. He would try to unsnap them and undo the zipper. I always wore either blue jeans or cords. He never tried to pull them off, he just undid them. He would feel my breasts with

174

one hand and put the other hand in my pants. His hand would be inside my underwear too. He most times had me laying on my back by this time. He would put his fingers inside my vagina. He would rub it and ask me if it was feeling good. I told him no. I told him to stop and I tried to pull his hand away.

Once this started, it would happen a couple of times a week, every week. This happened between Easter break and the end of school during 1985.

He would also at this time expose himself to me. He would unzip his own pants. He would take his penis out. He would want me to touch it. I told him no but sometimes he would take my hand and put it on his penis. His penis would be hard.

He would tell me to give him a blow-job. He exposed himself to me lots of times but only twice did he make me give him a blow-job. He used to hold onto my head. He hung on with two hands. He had one hand wrapped around each side of my head near my neck. I couldn't pull back. I used to tell him it was gross. I tried to pull away but couldn't because of the chesterfield. He would ask me not to tell. He said Alice wouldn't believe me and it would be my fault. When he had his penis in my mouth he asked me to suck on it.

I wouldn't and he used to say that I was doing it wrong. The first time I got out of it and left the room. The second time - the next night he tried it again.

Alice was home in bed both times. The second time he tried to move my head back and forth. I tried not to let him but he did some. He was kneeling. He started to ejaculate and loosened his grip on my head. I moved back. Part of it came in my mouth and part didn't.

I got up and walked quickly to the bathroom. I washed my mouth out. I went to my bedroom. I was crying.

He didn't say anything to me when I left. I thought he would come after me but he didn't.

I tried after this to stay in my room. Sometimes when Alice would go to bingo he would try to feel me if I was watching TV or walking around. He would make an odd pass now and then.

My bedroom door didn't have a lock on it and there was a block of wood preventing it from closing tight. Within a few days of the incidents on the couch he started to come into my bedroom. He would come in after Alice would go to Bingo. She went several times a week. I would be on my bed with my clothes on. Albert used to lean over the bed and undo his zipper. He would try to haul up my shirt but I would haul it down. He would expose himself. He would lay down on top of me. This happened quite a few times. He would rub himself against me. I would try to get away. He must have eventually realized he couldn't do anything so he gave up. He tried to kiss me but I wouldn't let him. He tried to put his hands in my pants but they were too tight so he couldn't. He would also, if he could, pull my brassiere up and feel my breasts. He never ejaculated during this. Several times he said he was going to take my cherry. I didn't know what it meant when he said it.

Once just before June exams (1985) Alice went out in the morning. I'm not sure what day it was. She left at about 8 AM. David was at his aunt's house, I think he had stayed over night there. I was in bed. I had been asleep and woke when I heard her leave. A while after she left Albert came into my bedroom. I was in bed under the covers in a night gown. I was wearing my under wear. Albert had only his under wear on. It was light enough that I could see him well. He walked over and pulled the covers back down near my knees.

He laid on the bed facing me. I was on my back. I was scared of what was coming next, I didn't say anything. He kept saying that this time he was going to get my cherry. He started to feel me. He took up my nightdress. I didn't have my brassiere on. He was feeling my breasts. He pulled my underwear down. I tried to pull it back up but couldn't. He had got on top of me already.

He took his underwear off just before he got on top of me. He had one hand on my breast. With his other hand he was trying to put his penis into my vagina. I couldn't move because he was on top of me. My underwear - panties- had come all the way off. I tried to hold my legs together. He pushed them apart and was laying between my legs. He told me I was too tight but he was still going to get my cherry. Both of his hands were up on my breasts. I could feel his penis in my vagina. He pushed on me several times. It went in but not all the way. He said it wasn't all the way in. He used both his hands to open me up and try to push his penis in further. It didn't work. I was telling him to stop. He asked my why. I told him because I didn't want him to do it. I told him I didn't want to get pregnant. He said he wouldn't let go inside of me. I struggled and pulled away from him.

He got up. I had my eyes closed. I didn't want to look at him. He left my bedroom. He went to the bathroom and ran a bath. When he got off the bed he said I was too tight. He had his bath.

I sat on the edge of the bed while he had his bath. When he was finished I went in and washed. When I was going in the bathroom and he was coming out he said, 'Maybe next time,' and to make sure I didn't tell Alice.

Shortly after that I had my grade eleven exams. I left for the summer shortly after this. I came back in September (1985). I spent less time at the Weller home and as much as I could at Mary Odell's place. I stayed until the school year was finished. I made sure I was never alone with Albert and he never made any more advances.

In June of 1986 I left Weller's. I went back and picked up my things in September. I have only made occasional visits back. Never stayed overnight since.

It was dated August 17, 1988, and signed by Ann Wicks, Constable Green, Edith Decker and Cindy Wilbur. It is the single most important document in this book. Because of it the RCMP finally had a case against Albert Weller. It led to the closure of his foster home and revelations of sexual abuse beyond the shroud of silence held so long in place by many people. The truth was finally heard in a manner that could no longer be silenced.

Ann wiped her tears away and immediately asked Green, "What will happen next?"

He was evasive, though truthful, "Well, I have to speak with my superiors. A complete C237 Report must be forwarded to the Department of Justice. They will read this statement and my report before they decide what to do."

Green noted that Ann was visibly upset throughout. She was concerned and asked him what would now happen with the investigation. She was very naive about some of the things she was describing and did not understand some of the sexual terminology.

Green had difficulty believing parts of her story. He had to ask himself how a girl could silently be sexually abused in one room, when the foster mother was in the next room. He could not understand her silence. He did not see Ann as a good witness in a court room, especially under cross-examination.

He wrote in his report:

> Feel we have a VERY difficult case to prove. Ann is an introvert. She had to be coaxed through the entire process. She broke down and cried every time an embarrassing remark was made. She would never hold up in a court situation.

He warned Ann that a mischief charge would probably be laid if it turned out that she was lying. Ann stuck by her story.

Green discussed the statement with Edith Decker before he left that evening. These two people were now in charge of the investigation. They had at their disposal two powerful agencies whose present object was to discover and stop situations of sexual abuse of foster children. One was the RCMP and the other was the Department of Social Services.

Cindy Wilbur left with Ann. Green and Decker met in her office at the Shipley Social Services Department.

"Well, now that you've got a statement the police investigation can begin," Edith said.

"Are the two girls still living in the foster home?" asked Green.

"Yes. I was out to the home Friday past. I spoke with the girls and they told me they were fine."

"So do you think the foster father is abusing either one of them?"

"No. The girls sleep in the same room and they told both me and Madonna Hynes that everything was fine. We spoke to them individually and alone."

"Did you tell the Wellers that an allegation had been made?"

"Yes. Madonna told them and they were shocked. I discussed it again with Alice Weller on Friday. She feels that it is a horrible mistake and says she can protect the girls if it should ever really happen."

"So you feel the girls are OK?" Green asked.

"Yes I do. I'll have to go out there again after what we've just heard from Ann, but I see no immediate danger."

"Neither do I," said Constable Green.

"I'll get in contact with you as soon as I visit the Wellers," said Decker.

"Oh, I won't be in the office until late next week. I'm taking some time off."

Green left the Shipley office and got in his police car for the drive back to Baywood. It was just after 8 p.m. and still bright in the long Newfoundland evenings of August. Not as hot as Alberta, he thought, but nice in August. In fact, August was the only month fit to live in this province. Someone had once told him that there are really only two seasons in Newfoundland. One is August and the other is rain, drizzle and fog.

He was looking forward to his time off. He had arrived from Bow River, Alberta just a month before. The time off would give him a chance to get settled into his new home.

It was 9 p.m. on August 17th, when Edith Decker looked at her crowded desk and thought about the hundred or more cases she had to deal with. She started to clue things up for the day. What a thing to face on the first week back from leave, she thought.

Neither Decker nor Green discussed the possibility of a joint approach by their agencies. Nor was their any consideration given to gaining or losing the element of surprise in the RCMP investigation of Albert Weller. No officer was to accompany Edith to the Weller house to either question Albert or observe his reaction to his accuser. Neither was he to be arrested, surveillanced, or the girls removed. The next chapter describes how the powers that be reacted to the situation in the Weller home.

CHAPTER 10

RCMP AND SOCIAL SERVICES REACT

The wheels of the gods grind slowly but they
grind exceedingly fine.

Ancient Greek proverb

Social worker Edith Decker knew more than she told. She
knew that Ann's statement to Constable Green was not the whole
story of the girl's sexual abuse. As disturbing as Ann's statement
was, the full truth was more disturbing. The whole truth involved
much more sexual activity than Ann was willing to reveal to
Green on August 17, 1988. As well, more people than Albert
Weller were involved. As the social workers discussed the case,
Cindy Wilbur revealed that Ann had feared she was pregnant at
least once while she was at Wellers. As Karen Khan concluded
in her report:

> ... this would not be the case if sexual
> intercourse had not actually taken place. In
> Edith Decker's opinion, her statement to the
> police did not cover all earlier discussions
> with Cindy Wilbur.

In other words, it appeared that Ann had told Cindy Wilbur
more than she told Green. This phenomenon, which may be
called partial disclosure or selective disclosure, or incremental

disclosure, occurred throughout this book. All four girls in this book exhibited the behaviour.

One of the first examples of it was Dawn Williams who initially had told the RCMP that Levi Weller had *physically* abused her. The twelve year old thought that admitting physical abuse was less embarrassing than sexual abuse and would be enough to stop her abuser. This backfired when the observant officer noted no bruises or marks and did not believe the child.

It must be realized that being a sexual abuse victim carries a stigma in our society, a stigma these girls are reluctant to embrace. The victims pick and chose how much they need to tell, striking a delicate balance between what will stop their tormentor, protect others, and yet not shame themselves and their families.

Ann Wicks, it should be remembered, only disclosed physical abuse against her first foster home. Ann selectively disclosed to the RCMP sexual abuse at the Weller home, without admitting that she had been completely penetrated by Albert Weller or sexually abused by anyone else. Ann's more recent disclosures to the Supreme Court describe a much more frightening level of abuse in both her foster homes.

It must be noted that the victims in this brief study did not disclose the full extent of all abuse by all the abusers at their first disclosure. They decided, consciously or unconsciously, when they were ready to do so. Often this appeared to be in increments of increasing severity. The completeness of the disclosures may depend on the level of trust, the reaction, the need to disclose, and the pressures to conceal.

Unfortunately this may suggest deceit, or half truths, but each victim is proceeding at an individual pace of recollection, comfort and ability. Possibly, some victims will never be able to discuss their sexual abuse.

There is another phenomena that occurred in these cases that also promotes selective disclosure: Victims sometimes refuse to remember incidents which they cannot deal with at a conscious level. They honestly have forgotten incidents too painful to remember.

For example, Dawn Williams, only later in life remembered being abused at even earlier ages than she first thought. This may be partly the reason for the American statistics which claim that less than 10% of victims report abuse while they are still children. The vast majority of disclosures come from them later when they are adults.

As well, partial, selective or incremental disclosure can be prompted by a desire to protect others. Ann may have withheld information to protect Alice Weller and Alicia Rollings, the nurse in who she first confided, both of whom she cared about very much.

So, Ann could justify her partial disclosure to Constable Green. She could reason: the abuser will be investigated by the RCMP, the girls in the home will be protected and the abuse will stop -maximize the positive. No need to disclose further - minimize the negative.

THURSDAY, AUGUST 18, 1988

Now the RCMP and Social Services could have swung into full gear to address the problem in the Weller foster home. They had a signed allegation of sexual assault from Ann Wicks.

Cindy Wilbur told the Hughes Commission that she had felt the statement alone justified removal of the two girls from the foster home. She told Hughes that she had expressed this to "the child welfare workers", the "case workers". These were Edith Decker and Madonna Hynes.

On Thursday, August 18, 1988, Edith Decker phoned her boss, Karen Khan at Regional Office. They went over the statement Ann had made the previous day. Khan wrote:

> It was agreed that we should not do anything to hamper the police investigation and they should be given every opportunity to interview Albert Weller to determine whether or not charges would be laid.

TUESDAY, AUGUST 23, 1988

Five days later, on Tuesday, August 23, Edith Decker phoned RCMP offices in Baywood. Constable Green was still on holidays, so she spoke to Sergeant Hilton. At this point records differ as to what was actually said. Social Services records state that Edith asked Hilton when the RCMP investigation would be taking place and when Albert would be interviewed:

"... she was advised 'they had other cases to attend to' and when she informed him as to our concern regarding the two children and her intention to speak to Albert Weller, Hilton stated 'to go ahead and do what you have to'."

It would be fair to say that there was a lack of cooperation between these two agencies at this point in the investigation.

Hilton indicated to the Social Workers that he had no problem with their going ahead and interviewing Albert Weller with regard to Ann's statement. "There was no indication as to whether this would hamper their future investigation."

Karen Khan quotes herself in her report to the Director as saying at this point: "This was discussed with K. Khan who once again stated we need to be concerned for the protection of the two children ..."

WEDNESDAY, AUGUST 24, 1988

On Wednesday, August 24, Green was back at the RCMP office in Baywood. According to his entry in the Report, he noted Edith Decker's message to call her but did not return her call during the day. Later that night he called her at home but there was no answer.

At 10 a.m. that same day Edith Decker met with Alice Weller at the Social Services office in Shipley. She confronted Alice with Ann's full statement. She pointed out the places and times the abuse was alleged to have occurred.

Alice was agitated and full of disbelief. She said, "I can't believe that could have happened in the living room. Our bedroom is just across the hall and I always sleep with the door open. I would have seen it or heard it."

"Did you and Albert discuss the allegations?"

"Of course. Albert told me, 'If they say that I abused Ann, they may as well say I abused my own sister'."

Contrary to available RCMP records, the Social Services

files indicate that Edith reached Constable Green by phone that afternoon. She supposedly advised him of the interview with Alice and Alice's steady defence of her husband. According to the Social Services report, Green suggested that Albert and Ann take a polygraph test.

THURSDAY, AUGUST 25, 1988

On Thursday, August 25, the RCMP diary record in Baywood contains another note from the perspicacious Officer Michael Dutois which ended with the prudent direction: "Albert Weller to be interviewed."

Unfortunately this would not occur for another 12 days.

Green wrote that he called Edith Decker at her home and office at 6 p.m. There was, he noted, no answer.

At 8 p.m. he reached Edith to return her call of August 23. He noted that there was nothing important in their conversation:

"She didn't want anything in particular only to ask if we'd managed to see Albert Weller yet. She was updated."

The only update was that he had not yet interviewed Albert Weller. Green did not see Edith Decker and the Department of Social Services as important colleagues in his RCMP investigation. He pursued little meaningful collaboration with them.

Later, Green told Justice Hughes that he could not recall any concern from the social worker that the interview with Albert Weller should occur "sooner rather than later". He was vague when asked if Officer Dutois had told him verbally to get on with the interview of Weller.

The Social Services Report on the activities of August 25, ends with the statement, "Still no information from RCMP when they were going to initiate their investigation." The past tense of the verb indicates that the comment may have been written sometime after the fact.

The RCMP continuing files on this case are strangely quiet from this date until the day that Tammy died. The sad fact is that the only active investigation, as ineffectual as it was, was done by the social workers and not by the RCMP.

FRIDAY, AUGUST 26, 1988

On Friday, August 26, Edith Decker went out to the Weller home to interview Albert and Alice. She took Albert through some of the details of the accusations by Ann Wicks. He denied everything. He couldn't believe that Ann had made these allegations. He broke down and cried.

The husband and wife took Edith through their home and showed how the living room was across the hall from the master bedroom. Alice claimed to be a light sleeper and would have heard any noises. Edith was met with adamant denials all round.

Tammy and Maggie were not interviewed that day as they were not at home during Edith's visit. So Edith Decker did not question nor remove the two sisters on that day. Edith reported that, "Alice Weller assured her that she was able to protect Tammy and Maggie."

Now begins a strange gap or hiatus in this case. The Social Services Report explains that Edith was busy with other cases all through the next week to Friday, September 1:

> Monday - Thursday, August 29, 30, 31, & Sept.1: E. Decker was unable to make contact with the Weller family due to other workload commitments including a court hearing ...

Then the following, unexplained, "Friday, September 2, 1988: E. Decker on annual leave - No one assigned to her caseload."

It appears that both principal agents of the RCMP and Social Services took holidays just after the allegation had been made by Ann on August 17. In neither case do the available records show that their work on the Weller foster home was continued in any meaningful way by other officials.

Edith Decker had just returned from educational leave on August 10, to depart again three weeks later on September 2. Green had just started work in Newfoundland in mid July, was assigned to the case August 1, and took time off August 19, just two days after Ann had made her emotional and crucial statement.

Even Edith's boss, Karen Khan, went on annual leave in

August and did not return until September 9, two days after Tammy's death.

The girls were on their own with their foster father. The fox was guarding the hen house.

TUESDAY, AUGUST 30, 1988

On August 30, Sergeant Don Hilton sent a telex to RCMP Criminal Operations in St. John's concerning the case. He related the allegations Ann had made 13 days before:

"... fondling and increased to forcible oral sex and one attempt at intercourse."

Hilton pointed out that the alleged victim had since left the home. He neglected to mention that two other girls were presently living in the home with the accused. He wrote:

"The matter is presently being investigated and suspect will be interviewed."

It was decided that no formal synopsis, called a C237, of the case was to be sent to RCMP Criminal Operations in St. John's, just a telex. This decision was the last recorded entry in the continuing report by the Baywood RCMP until September 6.

September 6 was the eventful day that the wind of discovery rustled among the concealed embers of the Weller foster homes and ignited a conflagration.

There was one other strange note in the RCMP report. There was a scrawl, running sideways on the RCMP report and underlined twice. In handwriting yet to be identified, were the two words: "EXPLAIN DELAY".

The unexplained delay was between Ann's detailed statement of sexual abuse given on August 17 and Green's eventual appearance at the home on September 6, 1988. This was a delay of 20 calendar days, even though he knew that two teenage girls were living with the alleged abuser, Albert Weller.

TUESDAY, SEPTEMBER 6, 1988

On Tuesday, September 6, two things happened that finally made the embers ignite: One was a phone call and the other was a visit.

The Social Services report states that in spite of the fact that Edith Decker had been assigned to the "child abuse unit," presumably at the Janeway, she made time that morning to phone Constable Green. She asked if he had started his investigation. Specifically, the question was if he had interviewed Albert Weller.

Green advised that he had not but would be doing so "later on in the week". He made no mention of this phone call in his own Continuation Report. Under questioning before Justice Hughes, Green admitted that it "is possible" that he spoke to Edith Decker in the morning of August, 6. He could not say if her call prompted him to visit the Albert Weller home later that same day.

In any case, Constable Green did turn up at the Weller house at 1:30 p.m. that afternoon to interview Albert. It was now twenty days since he had gotten the statement from Ann Wicks and it turned out to be a most propitious visit. During those twenty days, Tammy and Maggie King had continued to live in the foster home with the alleged sexual abuser.

Green found that Albert was not at home. Ironically, it was Albert Weller's last day of seasonal work as a park ranger at Square Pond Park. Alice Weller was interviewed by the constable for almost three hours. He informed her that there was an RCMP investigation of her husband as a result of the serious charges made by Ann Wicks.

For Alice Weller, the situation had taken on an entirely new dimension with the arrival of Constable Green. No longer was it a matter of community embarrassment or loss of the reputation of their foster home. No longer was it a private matter between her and the social workers. With the RCMP cruiser parked in her yard for three hours on August 6, things had changed utterly.

In Alice's mind "the penny dropped" as she listened to the young police officer with the large glasses and the small hands. In those hands Green held the signed and witnessed statement of Ann Wicks. It told of repeated sexual assaults by Albert in graphic words Alice had rarely heard.

This problem was not going away with a threatening letter from her lawyer, or a loyal defence of her husband. Green took no formal statement, but he read Ann's allegation and discussed it with Alice.

"I don't believe this," Alice Weller said at her kitchen table as she heard about Ann's statement.

"It is exactly as she told it," remarked the officer. "We will have to proceed with an investigation after allegations like that."

"Albert told me that none of it took place." She looked at the accusing sheets of paper in the officer's hands.

"Perhaps you were asleep when it happened."

Alice shook her head, "No, I'm a light sleeper. I would have heard it."

"Perhaps you weren't home."

"I never even saw anything suspicious going on. Ann says everything happened here in the house. If she had said it happened when she and Albert were alone at the cabin in Deep Harbour Pond, I might have believed her."

"What do you mean?"

"The two of them were out to the cabin a number of times, but Ann didn't say anything happened out there. It just doesn't make sense to me."

"Did you talk with the two girls presently in the home?"

"Yes I spoke with them both and they said nothing happened."

Once again, Alice neglected to mention Frank Weller's assault alleged earlier by Maggie, and later proved in court.

Green left at 4 p.m. but not before making an appointment to speak with Albert and Alice at RCMP headquarters the next morning at 10 a.m. It was an appointment that neither of them would keep.

Alice Weller was thoroughly upset by the RCMP visit. She had already been having some doubts about her husband's innocence. Thoughts of what his guilt implied tormented her ceaselessly, but she refused to let her mind go further down that road.

On the previous Sunday, September 4, driven by desperation and confusion, she had phoned Ann Wicks. Alice wanted to hear from her former foster daughter's own lips the accusations that her husband Albert was a sex abuser.

To her chagrin, that is essentially what she heard from Ann in their telephone conversation.

The RCMP were at the door and Alice Weller realized that she may have been mistaken about her husband's innocence.

She looked up to see her son David walk into the kitchen.

"Mom, when's supper?"

"David come here."

He could see his mother's agitated condition. "What's wrong, Mom? Someone said there was a police car in our yard."

"The RCMP were here and they say that your father sexually abused Ann."

Alice put her hands over her face and the tears fell into her fingers. With the truth out Alice noticed that David had not responded to the shocking revelation.

"David, do you know anything about your father and Ann?"

"Yes." Then he too began to cry.

"Well for God's sake tell me what it is."

She was reaching across to him with her hands and shaking his shoulders as if to shake the cold, hard truth at last out onto their kitchen floor.

"I saw Dad and Ann together."

"What do you mean together?"

Through his tears to her tears the simple, vulgar truth arrived:

"I saw Dad in her bedroom. She was lying face down on her bed and he had his hand up in under her night dress. She was crying."

Like a child picking a sore, Alice pursued the painful facts. "Did you ever see him with Tammy?"

She was not surprised by his answer, just numbed. The simplicity of it was jarring. His mother's gaze was distracted. He was expecting a reaction of some kind. She just looked over his head into the kitchen wall towards Square Pond Park where her marriage had just ended. It was as if Albert had suddenly released his end of a long rope between them and she felt herself falling backwards. She felt abandoned, rudderless, lost.

"Mom?" he asked.

She uttered not a word, but stared like a crazy woman who did not see him. David got up and walked back out the door.

Albert soon returned from his last day at work, less than an hour after Constable Green had left the house.

Since his work was seasonal, Albert would not necessarily have been feeling badly that he had finished for another season. He was, no doubt, concerned about the sexual assault allegations made by Ann Wicks. The possibility of an RCMP investigation and subsequent arrest also loomed on the horizon.

But Albert knew he had at least two things going for him up till then. There had been no witness to the abuse, so it was Ann's word against his. He would be presumed innocent until someone could prove him guilty. Also, he had a loyal wife who believed him and was stalwart in her defence of him.

The warm days of summer still lingered. In Square Pond Park, there already had been occasional cold winds and days where the overcast sky sent shivers through Albert's park ranger's uniform. The closing of the provincial parks in September signalled the end of the visiting tourists from the mainland. It also signalled the imminent arrival of cooler autumn weather. As he drove out though the gate of the park for the last time, he could see that the deciduous trees still retained their silver and green. No red or gold banners yet signalled the bitter arrival of the windy forces of autumn.

He may have been contemplating these things as he drove his jeep up the small lane leading to his house. The fall leaves had not yet begun to drop. The spirit of summer appeared to be still firmly in charge. But everything in his life was about to change.

As Albert walked into his house and planked down his lunch pail, he immediately knew that something was wrong. Even before he walked across the kitchen floor to get a beer from the fridge, he knew it. The signs were everywhere, screaming at him: TROUBLE.

There was no familiar smell of supper on the table or on the stove. There was no word of greeting, and he could tell by the way Alice stood with her back to him that she was getting ready to confront him with something.

"The Mounties were here today." She was at the sink with a half finished cup of tea going cold on the counter.

"Oh yeah?" He hardly seemed interested.

"They've started their investigation of you and Ann."

"You know I didn't do anything wrong; we've been through all that before with the social workers."

He opened a beer and took a long drag from the up-turned bottle.

"I know you <u>did</u> do it," she was facing him now.

His look was milder than hers, but firm. "No, Alice, I honestly didn't."

She looked into the eyes of the man she had loved and married 'for better or for worse till death', the father of her only son. His eyes held hers softly. She wanted to believe him.

Suddenly she pulled herself back from the tempting lie and faced the pain of the truth like a smack in her face. She turned back to the sink.

"I know because David saw you at it with Ann."

"What?"

"He saw you both in on the bed and you were feeling up in under her night dress."

Her arms held her up as she firmly gripped the arbourite counter top by the sink. He could not see her white knuckles as her back was turned to him.

"Albert, were you at it with Tammy, too?"

His silence told her everything.

She turned around to face him. "You make me sick."

The strength of her feelings, newly formed, began to direct themselves at him. Her eyes opened wide and her teeth clenched out the words of condemnation and betrayal.

Later, she could not remember exactly what she said to him. But it was all about lies and the end of their marriage and her never wanting to see him again.

The next thing she clearly remembered was being alone in the kitchen sipping on a cold cup of tea. Her hands were shaking, but not a lot, and he was gone. The clock on the wall said 5 p.m.

"Hi, Alice, what did the Mounties want? They were saying at the store that the Mounties were in our yard."

The voice was Tammy's.

She was home from her first day in school for the year. It was also to be her last. Tammy walked into the kitchen and sat at the table. She wore well-fitting, blue jeans and running shoes. Her big dark eyes with the long lashes were inquiring but friendly.

Alice pounced on her with a question, "Tammy did Albert ever touch you sexually?"

The suddenness of the question dumbfounded the girl. She stared as if addled. Alice laid the tea cup on the counter top and walked across to the table.

"Were you involved with Albert?" She looked down into the large, gaping brown eyes.

"Were you?"

"No." Tammy's eyes ferreted around the room as if looking for something to focus on.

"Tammy! You tell me and you tell me right now." Alice turned to a lie to prompt the girl to tell the truth, "The RCMP were here and they said they were going to give you the lie detector test, so you better tell me now."

Then Tammy blurted out the first of the almost accurate truth.

"I couldn't tell you. It would shock you too much. You were his wife and I didn't want to hurt you. I knew it would hurt you very much."

"Yes, it does," Alice said, quietly.

"He said no one would believe me, and even if they did, we'd just be moved to a group home. No one wants kids our age; everyone wants real young foster kids that they can raise as their own."

Terror and sadness filled the girl's eyes.

Alice looked at her blankly. "Then, it is all true, just as Ann said in her statement."

"You must hate me."

"And he was doing it with you, too? Just like Ann?"

Tammy stopped in mid thought. Her eyes became clear and thoughts focused. "No, it was not like with him and Ann."

"What do you mean?" asked the confused wife.

"It wasn't like him and Ann. It was different."

Alice felt the hurt and betrayal more than she had imagined possible.

"Tammy, he was a married man. He was using you."

"No. I love him. I'll kill myself if we're ever found out."

"Tammy, what about me? I'm his wife."

Tammy looked at Alice. "You must hate me."

195

Alice did not, but she could feel reason and logic flying away in all directions. There was no sense any more. She felt overwhelmed by her emotions, drowning in a sea of feelings which she could not sort out. Opposite her sat a girl drowning in the same sea. Tammy's chest heaved as she sobbed gently.

"This is a horrible! What will we do?" Alice said.

"I'll kill myself before I go into a group home, Alice." Tammy was suddenly lucid and resolved. "I won't let them put me in a group home, no matter what Albert and I did."

Alice walked back to the stove and boiled the kettle for another cup of tea.

She tried to stretch her mind to encompass all she now knew. She tried to understand the end of her marriage, the abuse of her foster children, the whispering in the community, the future.

When she looked up from her thoughts Tammy was gone. She looked into the girl's bedroom and saw Tammy face down on the bed. Alice gently closed the bedroom door.

She was still drinking tea when Maggie bounced into the kitchen. Maggie too realized immediately that something was wrong as soon as she saw Alice.

Maggie remembers noticing no supper, no Albert, Tammy or David. She went to the kitchen table and sat down. Alice was standing up in the middle of the kitchen.

"Maggie, you get your own supper tonight. No one else is hungry and no one else is going to be eating."

"Oh, all right." Maggie fixed herself a peanut butter sandwich.

Breaking the quiet, Maggie asked, "Where's Albert?"

"Albert won't be coming home any more."

Maggie had a horrible sinking feeling. What she feared most was trouble. Trouble meant she no longer had control over her life. Trouble meant she could stay or be placed somewhere else. Trouble could mean a dreaded group home.

"Where's Tammy?"

"In her room."

"What's wrong?"

A bitterness came into Alice's voice. "Go ask Tammy what's wrong. Tammy can tell you all about it."

When Maggie walked into the bedroom Tammy was sitting on the floor by her bed. She was writing with her head down.

"What's going on?" the thirteen year old asked her sister.

Tammy looked up and Maggie could see her eyes were red from crying.

"What's happening, Tammy?" Maggie could feel the panic rising inside her like a flood that was beginning to engulf her, smother her. She shrieked, "What's happening to us?"

But Tammy looked down again. She continued to write what appeared to be letters in the large note pad on her lap. "You wouldn't understand," she told her younger sister.

"What is it?"

"It's out of our control now." Her eyes looked up and at the window. It seemed she was focused on a distant hill. "Out of control," she repeated.

Maggie went over to where Tammy sat on the floor by the bed. She sat down with her and looked at what Tammy was writing. It was a series of letters to her brother, sisters and parents. The one on top was to their sister Liza. Over Tammy's shoulder, Maggie could read:

"Dear Liza, I am sorry I never got the chance to know you better ..."

Later that night when Maggie was alone she went through the letters and she noticed that they were all written as if Tammy were not expecting to see her family again.

The two sisters sat on the floor of their bedroom with their backs to Tammy's bunk. They sat together for the last time, in silence as late summer darkness fell on the small bungalow.

Outside, the eternal seasons were changing about their heads as imperceptibly as a rising tide, or a sinking sun. The evening dew settled invisibly on the needles of the pines and ubiquitous spruce trees surrounding their house.

The rarer birch and poplar stood scattered past the houses in by Willie's Pond. Invisible changes were already occurring inside their skin-like bark. The inscrutable leaves told no tale, but the sap was already starting to sink from their branches down to their roots. These sensitive deciduous trees knew something that the hearty evergreens did not. Winter was coming! They remembered the cold blasts and shivered in the open fields near Willie's pond.

Overhead the simple stars peeped and blinked. The last sliver of the old moon peered occasionally from between ominous black clouds that flew low over the horizon. These heavy black clouds seemed to bump the land occasionally like drunken teenage revellers in large cars. If the heavens were aware of the impending tragedy, they showed no sign of it on Tuesday night, September 6, 1988.

The heavens moved with clouds, moon and stars but were just as indifferent to the events in Albert Weller's house as the silent, 450 million year old cliffs of Gros Morne Park. The big earth turned on its axis with the deliberateness of time. At the poles the ice was melting, the last ice age ending as silently as it had begun. But none of those things heeded Tammy or appeared mindful of her plight on this, the eve of her death.

Albert Weller looked up at the sky from the door of his cabin in Deep Harbour Pond. Albert was a man who liked his privacy and tonight he had it. The peeping stars helped him forget his troubles as he took a deep draught of beer. He would figure it all out tomorrow, he reasoned.

Maggie sat beside her older sister on their bedroom floor and silently contemplated their suddenly uncertain future. They sat together silently for what may have been hours. Suddenly she heard her own voice say, "Tammy, I love you."

Tammy looked up at her. "What?"

"No matter what happens, I love you."

"Oh, you know I love you too, Maggie."

Tammy reached over and took her younger sister into her arms and hugged her warmly. Maggie cried into Tammy's shoulder and when she looked she saw tears in Tammy's eyes too.

"You usually say you hate me when we fight," Tammy laughed through her tears.

Maggie remembered how Tammy would always answer, "Well, I don't hate you."

"Not any more," Maggie said. "I'll never say that to you again."

"Come out and tell Alice," Tammy said. Then, so delighted,

she went out of the bedroom to tell Alice how Maggie had said she loved her. It was a little oasis of joy in a desert of trouble.

Maggie could hear her in the kitchen saying: "You know who just said she loves me? Maggie."

"Well that's a switch," Alice said.

Tammy and Maggie spent the rest of their last evening together in their room. They stayed up until late, chatting.

The next morning Maggie got up at eight o'clock to get ready for school. She was dressed and ready to go through the bedroom door when she noticed that Tammy was awake. She was propped up on her elbow on her lower bunk looking at Maggie, but not speaking.

Maggie told her older sister, "Lie down and go to sleep. You don't have to go to school today, remember. You registered yesterday. It's just for the Junior High today."

"OK, good-bye."

"Good-bye." Maggie closed the bedroom door behind her as she left. That was the last time she saw her sister, Tammy, alive.

CHAPTER 11

NOT A DAY FOR DYING

Who killed cock robin?
Not I said the sparrow
With my little arrow ...

English folk rhyme

Wednesday, September 7, 1988 did not seem like a day for dying in Deep Harbour. It was sunny and warm with a soft, pine scented, westerly wind off the land.

John Dobbin woke early. He carefully swung his feet out onto the floor so as not to wake his wife sleeping quietly beside him. He thought about the box for the graveyard he had promised to build with his brother Bob. The wood was all ready in Bob's garage.

Albert Weller awoke and looked out his cabin door. The sun was steaming the water of the pond with a mist as the warmer air from the land met the cool damp air on the water.

The warm morning sun shone on a clean green land of "pine clad hills" as Alice Weller opened her back door and looked out at her world. Past generations of Newfoundlanders usually faced the sea, but more recent, non-fishing communities were just as happy to face their houses to the land away from the shore.

The sun was just beginning to lick the dew from the long brown grass and the green spruce needles. The windows and all things not yet touched by the sun were still cool and damp. The air was deliciously cool and exhilarating; Alice breathed deeply.

After finally and fretfully falling to sleep late the previous night she had slept well. But now her troubles suddenly came back to her like a smack in the face. She closed the door and went back into the house where the dreariness of the night still persisted.

The sun, too, still persisted across the land. Soon the door opened again and Maggie King walked out, pretty in her new clothes, to meet the bus for school. Tammy got up briefly, then went back to bed.

In nearby Baywood the sun shone just as warmly on the RCMP offices. It was Wednesday morning, a business day as officers attended the files for which they were responsible.

The large clock on the wall eventually showed that the 10 a.m. appointment of Albert and Alice Weller had come and gone. Neither of them showed, but Constable Green did not respond to this, as he was engaged in other matters.

According to what Alice told Social Services:

> Tammy got up again at approximately
> 11 a.m., ate breakfast, washed the dishes, and
> supposedly left the home at 1 p.m. to go next
> door to feed the chickens.

Alice's son David went to Deep Harbour Pond to see if the family jeep was there. He returned later that morning to inform his mother that it was, unlocked.

The road ended beside the pond and the cabin was on an island, shouting distance from shore. This was approximately five or six kilometres south west of the Albert Weller house, away from the community and into the woods. It was a brisk one hour walk.

Just after 3 p.m. Maggie arrived from school. "Where's Tammy?" she asked.

According to Maggie, Alice answered, "I guess she's at Sherri Driscoll's. She got up and left and she didn't say where she was going this morning ..."

Alice was making arrangements for someone to drive her to Deep Harbour Pond to retrieve the family jeep.

But Tammy did not go to Sherri Driscoll's nor to feed the ducks next door. When she left the house at about 1 p.m., she walked the six kilometres to the Deep Harbour Pond cabin to be with Albert Weller. Had she and Alice argued, fought? Had she left quietly or in the heat of anger?

What thoughts were in her confused head as she walked alone over the same secluded paths where she and Albert had often walked together? She saw where they had stopped and talked. The dirt road was little more than a path as it reached the pond.

She immediately saw where he had parked the jeep and in the distance she saw the cabin.

Albert had arrived at the cabin late the previous evening. He had gone to the liquor store where he purchased at least a dozen beer and a large bottle of wine. He had drunk but not eaten that night as he contemplated his problems alone into the night.

Wednesday morning he had gotten up at about eight with all his troubles still intact. Now he had a hangover as well. His job had ended, as well as his marriage and probably his relationship with Tammy. Worse yet everyone would soon know his secrets.

He lit the stove in the cabin which soon dispelled the damp morning air. He went for a walk around the island, came back to the cabin and had a drink. He took in his hands a piece of rope. He tied a hangman's noose on the end and contemplated his future.

In the afternoon he was lying in his bunk when he heard shouting from a point of land opposite the island.

Albert described the scene to the judicial inquiry under Judge LeClair:

> I don't know the time ... but I heard someone singing out. There's a point that comes out in the pond, right. I didn't pay no attention to it and after a while they kept singing out and I knew by the voice it was Tammy.

She shouted out to him, "Albert! Albert!"
There was no answer.
"Albert! Come and get me in the boat."

The desperate words from the verge of ruin echoed across the summer pond. It was by now 2 p.m., Wednesday, September 7, 1988.

Albert told the police that he heard her shouting from the shore and he told her to go back home.

"Different times I told her to go home and she said no, I'm swimming out. And I knew in my heart and soul - I knew that she wouldn't make it. So I left with the boat and I went down and got her and I brought her back to the cabin."

Those are strange words to describe an excellent swimmer like Tammy.

Imagine the scene in that secluded cabin. The two of them lost in the chemistry of their doomed relationship. Unwise and undirected by good judgement, it had brought them to this pause on the edge of the abyss.

Neither had the sense or the understanding to handle the situation appropriately. They had raced with it downhill till it crashed into some grim realities, like of Albert's past as an abuser, and Alice's pathetic grief as his wife. The RCMP and the Social Services Department, long inert, were now hot on their trail.

Albert said that Tammy offered him her pay for the month at the town council project. She had just cashed her check at the store and he could see a fifty dollar bill. He refused it.

Lies come easily from all sources at this point. This chapter should be entitled "Caveat Emptor", or let the reader beware.

Albert, Alice, and most sources, prevaricate, dissemble, or put the facts in the shape that will best illustrate their most favourable reality.

Albert had much to fear from the truth. He was liable to charges of sexual assault against Tammy, and he was soon to be on trial for sexual assault against Ann when he spoke to Judge LeClair. This would cause the most frank of men to couch their remarks in self-preservation. Albert Weller was not the most frank of men:

"What did you do at the cabin?" asked the lawyer.

"She sat down and she was crying and everything."

"Why was she crying, do you know?"

"She told me what Alice made her do."

"What did Tammy tell you Alice made her do?"

"Well, she made her tell that I had sexual intercourse with her and all this.... She wouldn't believe the truth."

"And the truth is what?"

"That she didn't. That we didn't. She said everyone believes lies. Tammy said she was going to commit suicide. She said she was going to do it that night when she was home.

"How? Did she say?"

"Well, she said with pills. She said there were enough pills at home."

"What - I mean I find hard, you know, to believe, that Tammy - if there was nothing going on, how Alice could make her tell?"

"Yeah, but Tammy told me Alice frightened her."

"Threatened her with what?"

"Now I don't know. That's all the girl told me. I never asked her how she, because I wanted to get her mind off it. That's all she was talking about was committing suicide ... she was shivering and crying and shaking and she was in a bad state. She asked me could she have a drop of wine in a glass. I gave her about this much in a plastic glass."

"She calmed down, I calmed her down. And I told her, I said, Tammy - this is what I told her - I said Alice is not going to hurt you. Tammy said - yes she is.

I said no and I kept talking to her like that and I said no she won't. So I said I'll take you home and I'll drop you off and you can go on back to the house and I said everything will be OK."

"Now before we go on, Mr. Weller, there was some indication given earlier by Maggie that you often had said we are going to send you to a group home or something like that. What was that all about? Was there any conversation about a group home?

"I never said that."

"Well somebody said it because ..."

"Alice used to be talking about group homes and this is what Tammy used to say. She said I'll never end up in a group home."

"... Alice says that she didn't talk about a group home."

"Well I never told Tammy that she had to end up in a group home ..."

"Maggie says that you did."

"Well I didn't ... I told Tammy that she would never end up in a group home if I could possibly help it. And that's the truth."

"OK, so she had a glass or a bit of wine and you spent about an hour there."

"Yeah."

"Was there any physical contact?"

"No."

"You did not comfort her in any way."

"No, none what so ever."

"Was she an attractive girl?"

"Yes, she was attractive."

In any event, back at Deep Harbour, by about 3:30 p.m. Alice had secured the services of her brother-in-law, Pat Weller, to drive her in to Deep Harbour Pond. They drove the short but rough road in to the cabin, allegedly to retrieve the jeep.

Albert and Tammy were by that time driving out from the cabin, as he alleges, in order for him to bring Tammy home. He met Alice and his brother Pat in Pat's car on the narrow road from the pond.

The tragic situation had now reached "critical mass" and, like a nuclear reaction, had taken on a life of its own. Emotions and events were now beyond anyone's control, in total free fall. They were like rogue planets who had slipped from their orbits. Two of these planets then collided on the dirt road not far from the foot of Deep Harbour Pond.

Certain facts we know from a corroboration of unfriendly witnesses. Alice saw Albert and Tammy in their jeep and became very upset. In fact she became hysterical. She got out of Pat Weller's car and approached the jeep.

Suddenly all the anger, jealousy, hurt and frustration came rushing to the surface. Alice saw the horrible truth of Albert and Tammy. Side by side she saw them in the front seat of the jeep where she should ride with her husband.

She took a large stone from the ground and dashed it through the windshield of the jeep. Tammy screamed, "I want to get out of here," and Albert tried to get the jeep back on the narrow road past his brother Pat's car.

Alice took another rock and smashed it into the side window as Albert and Tammy drove by them and hurtled towards Deep Harbour, out of sight. It was then about 4:00 p.m. on Wednesday, September 7, 1988. That was the last time anyone except Albert saw Tammy King alive.

From external appearances it was still a beautiful day in Deep Harbour. The sun bobbed between fat cumulus clouds in a late summer sky. A slight westerly breeze blew. Some kids jigged tomcods from the local wharf. Down the harbour in a garage near the local church, two fishermen were silently building a wooden box for the graveyard.

Albert later described the situation for Judge Leclair:

> When they came up and my brother met me he slowed down and before the truck was stopped Alice was out and picked up the rock and put it through the windshield. And Tammy just went crazy screaming and everything else. And the other rock went through the side glass.

Later, at 4:18 p.m. that afternoon, a call was received at RCMP Baywood detachment from an emotional Alice Weller. Constable Dutois, who took the call, reported that she was distraught and that she wanted to speak to Constable Green.

Alice told Dutois that she now knew that the charges of sexual assault against her husband were true. She threatened to kill her husband and herself. She wanted to speak to the investigating officer, Green.

At that moment, Green was practically next door to Alice, investigating another sexual assault case. He had not followed up on the interview with Albert and Alice Weller scheduled for 10 o'clock that morning. He later told Justice Hughes, other cases had distracted and, "... took me away from inquiring as to why they hadn't come in."

Now the investigating officer was forced to play catch up. He arrived at the Weller house to find Alice quite different from his last visit. "Alice was found to be in a very agitated state." She told Constable Green "... that Albert was indeed guilty and that he had been involved sexually with both Ann and Tammy, a present foster child aged 15.... An immediate search was started for Albert and the foster girl."

RCMP Baywood detachment finally addressed the case with its undivided attention. Their investigation report details their strenuous exertions:

> An immediate search was undertaken by all available manpower in an attempt to locate Albert Weller and Tammy King. Corporal Newbury, the senior member at the Detachment was advised and co-ordinated the search. Sergeant Hilton, Detachment Commander, was advised of the incident at 1701 hours.

> A request was made for the services of St. John's EMO helicopter to do an air search of the area in an effort to locate the vehicle Albert had been driving. EMO helicopter was provided and searched for approximately one hour, until dark, at which time it returned to St. John's. Neither the vehicle nor Albert Weller nor Tammy King could be located.

One can almost hear the barn doors slamming as the horses gallop away. Tammy and Albert were two horses who galloped out the dirt road from Deep Harbour Pond. They soon reached the pavement of the main road and they took the highway for a brief while. They came to the dirt lane that leads towards Rocky Cove Point.

It is a short, winding road that soon loses itself in the thick woods after a kilometre or so. The road winds along the south east side of the harbour where it finally ends just short of reaching the water. One hundred meters of dense trees lead to the edge of the cliffs. Fifteen meters below, the cliffs abruptly meet the blue-grey water of the Atlantic Ocean at Deep Harbour.

Meanwhile, Alice Weller had reached either Edith Decker or Madonna Hynes by phone. The files of both RCMP and Social Services are often vague about exactly which of their members did what. The Social Services file reads: "Between 5 p.m. and 6:30 p.m. on September 7, 1988, Alice Weller advised E. Decker and M. Hynes that she talked to Maggie ..."

Did she phone them both? Were they both on the phone? Did one contact the other later? Who received Alice's call? Where?

The RCMP files are also sometimes vague. For example, their files state that the boat containing Tammy's body "was met at the wharf." No mention is made of the officer's name who was present on the wharf or who made the arrest. Nor did the unknown RCMP officer identify himself to the two fishermen who brought in the body.

In any event, the two social workers turned up at the Weller house at about 6:30 p.m. that same evening. The social workers were shocked to realize the new state of affairs: Albert and Tammy were fled, Alice distraught and the RCMP involved in a frantic search.

More troubling was the changed stories of Maggie and Alice. Maggie now said that all was not right at the foster home. She had had strong suspicions of a sexual relationship between Tammy and Albert for a long time.

"She had seen them go for walks together, stay up late to watch late shows, and knew that Tammy was carrying three pictures of Albert in her wallet ... She felt she was not wanted by Tammy and Albert."

The shocked social workers knew they were in deep now. They asked Maggie why she had lied to them so boldly when they first asked her these same questions three weeks before.

Maggie told them that she could prove nothing and she had not wanted to be taken out of the home and put in a group home.

"Alice Weller stated she then felt Tammy was with her husband willingly - why else would she have gone to the cabin? She felt Albert did not force himself on her."

The two social workers then removed Maggie from the home and, in fulfilment of the young girl's worst nightmare, placed her in a group home in St. John's.

Another barn door was slammed securely shut.

By this time, Tammy and Albert were on the short road to the water on Rocky Cove Point. The only living person who knows what really happened after that is Albert Weller. Below is what he swore under oath at the Leclair Inquiry. He is describing their flight from Alice's wrath immediately after the stone-throwing incident:

> And Tammy kept on saying drive, drive, drive, drive. I said I'm driving as fast as I could over that road. She said hide. And I said there's no place to hide... And when I came out to the highway I wanted to take her to the police station and she said definitely not.

"Why the police station, Mr. Weller?" (Questions asked by Senior Crown Prosecutor, Frank Gronich).

> Well I had no other place to go. This was the only thing playing on my mind. Just the girl was really crazy. I mean she was really going crazy. So, no, she wouldn't agree to it because she said she'd jump out.

"Out of the truck?"

> Out of the jeep, yeah. So when she wouldn't agree to that, I said, Tammy, I don't know where to go. I don't know what to do.

> She said keep driving. Hide the jeep somewhere. So all I could think of was my brother's piece of land on Rocky Cove Point... I used to be down there years ago. My father cut hay and when we were youngsters we used to go there all the time.

> And this was the only place I could

think of because it was all grew up, you know, with trees and everything. I went down there because she wouldn't stay in the jeep. I said, stay in it because it's getting chilly. She wouldn't because she said someone would see it and find us. She wanted to get down by the shore line and she went back and forth, back and forth.

Come on, I said, I can't keep up to you. Come back and we'll sit in the jeep and I'll turn the heat on. No, she wouldn't do it. "Then she got it in her mind that ... they were going to spot the jeep because she heard a helicopter.

Albert explained to the Court of Inquiry that she directed him to go back up the hill and hide the jeep. She wanted to stay in the trees by the water's edge. He did not trust her alone for fear she might try to kill herself. He told Judge LeClair:

... She was down in the trees and she wanted me to come up and hide the jeep but she wanted to stay there. But I wouldn't let her because I figured that she was going to do something. I caught her by the hand and I said come on up, you got to get in the jeep too.

So she got in the jeep and I put the jeep down over a little embankment you know, because she was a four wheel drive ...it was hidden under the trees, but she still wouldn't stay in the jeep.

...I couldn't keep her in the jeep. She wanted to go down...and sit down against the trees. So that's what we done. And she had on a white coat and she heard another helicopter.

...She heard a helicopter and she took off the white jacket. She said, they'd see that. She rolled it up and put it under her arm....and there was a blanket in the jeep and that's what we got and put it around her when she took off the coat.

Well, I stayed with her talking to her. I said come on, we'll get out of it...she wouldn't leave with me. She said, wait for another while...wait until it gets a bit dark so no one will see where we are going.

And in the trees was a little clearing, a grassy place. So when the helicopter was to the right of where we were standing, it kind of lowered down. And she said to me, ' Where is it? Where is it at? Where is it landing? '

I said, what odds about it. But no she wouldn't. She came out with me and I turned back and SHE TOOK OFF. And that was all.

I took off after her but I couldn't catch her. I told her to come back. She said something, I don't know what it was that she said. She went on, she dived, she jumped.

She jumped ...

Thus, Albert Weller, the only living witness, described Tammy's last desperate run to the edge of the cliff. In spite of his good advice to leave the scene with him, she stayed and jumped to her death. He did not even hear her final, stricken words to him shouted over her shoulder as she fell.

Her whole life had led her to the edge of this cliff. My search for her led me here too some months later.

The little flat shelf she jumped from is only the size of a

small desk top. It is perched atop the cliff at the edge of the trees. It is the only place within sight in both directions along the shore that a person could jump into the water without hitting cliff on the way down.

At this brief spot, the cliff is almost vertical, down 15 meters, or 44 feet, to the Atlantic. Forensic reports indicate that she hit the water on her left side almost head first. At the moment of impact, she would have been falling 16 meters per second, almost forty miles an hour. The shock of hitting the water from that height probably knocked her out and, without artificial resuscitation, she soon drowned.

Tammy died.

Death is probably not as bad for the participant as melodramatic people have made it out to be. The circumstances causing death can be painful emotionally and physically. The grief for those left behind is bad. But what of the experience of death itself?

In the last moments of her earthly life, Tammy probably found herself in the air falling towards the Atlantic. Her troubles with helicopters, group homes, foster homes, Albert, Alice and all human woes, fell away behind her and she tumbled like a parachutist leaving a burning, doomed plane.

Time probably slowed down as she was leaving it. She may have felt herself falling slowly, like Alice down the rabbit hole. Then she was floating out of her body.

She did not want to go back to face her accusers, like Alice and the others throwing their stones, calling her a prostitute with their eyes.

Poor Albert, was ineffectual and no help to her. Edith Decker and the social workers were not to be trusted. The RCMP were agents of the system, well meaning but no help either.

Most of all, she could not face the many eyes. The approaching night could not hide her for long. In the morning everyone's eyes would stare and become stones that would accuse her unwise love for Albert Weller. They would call her sinful, vile and bad. Those eyes would suddenly turn to stones and come crashing through whatever windshield hid her.

Why would she want to go back? To what?

Her parachute opened and she was saved.

Albert continued, "And she jumped and I jumped after her and I went down right to the bottom and when I came up I went down again. When I came up the second time I looked over my shoulder and she was about 10 feet from me lying face down in the water. So I scravelled, I can't swim, I scravelled and I got to her. I tried to turn her over but I couldn't. Every time I'd go to turn her over, I'd go down. I dragged her in but she was dead."

"How did you know she was dead?"

"I felt her pulse and I felt the pulse in her neck."

"Was any attempt made to resuscitate her, give her life (mouth to mouth)?"

"There was nothing...No, I never done that."

"Do you have any training in this regard?"

"A little, not very much."

"Well, I mean you're a forest ranger, is it?"

"Yeah, I took a course in it."

"If so, why didn't you make effort to possibly resuscitate her?"

"Well, I couldn't get no pulse or I couldn't get anything. She wasn't making a murmur."

"Wouldn't it be difficult to feel a pulse. You're in up to here in water and it's cold and you're cold. I would find it difficult to find a pulse on anybody."

"Well, I don't know. That's the only thing really I could think about at that time."

"How long do you think both of you were in the water?"

"I don't really know. It seemed like a long time. It seemed like, well, an hour to me. But it might be only fifteen minutes."

By Wednesday, September 7, 1988 the RCMP were making the case a top priority at last. In a frenzy of belated activity, they raced around Deep Harbour with police lights flashing and the emergency helicopter hovering ominously. But Tammy and Albert were not located by the RCMP. As we know, they were found by two fishermen who had been working on a monument for the local cemetery.

So it came to pass that John Dobbin and his brother Bob discovered this tragic frieze on Rocky Cove Point: A man up to his knees in water, perched on a ledge at the base of a cliff. One hand was behind him on the cliff face. The other was clutching the wrist of a young woman's inert body.

Constable Green's next note in the Continuation Report is at 8 p.m., September 7, 1988. It reads:

> Albert Weller was taken into custody as a result of the foster girl turning up dead with him. He was lodged in cells and then transported by ambulance after being seen by Doctor Waldo to Health Sciences Centre in St. John's where he was placed under guard.

Dr. John Waldo had observed that Albert was suffering from hypothermia and an irregular heart beat. Therefore Waldo sent him almost directly to hospital. No thorough interrogation occurred until later when Albert had a few days time to consult a lawyer and arrange his recollections.

A more immediate questioning of Albert Weller by the RCMP on the night of Tammy's death may have been more revealing. This assumes that RCMP Baywood had someone qualified to interrogate properly and prescient enough to realize the importance of a prompt and candid statement by the suspect. It also assumes that someone had time enough to do it.

> Albert Weller was interviewed in the Health Sciences Centre. A cautioned statement was taken from him in which he advised that Tammy King had jumped from the cliff in an apparent suicide attempt.

> He said he jumped in to try and save her but it was too late. Albert was questioned at this time about any sexual activity he may have had with Tammy King. He would not discuss this matter with the investigator and stated he wished to consult with a lawyer.

The doctors noted to the investigators that his cuts and scrapes were consistent with sliding down the cliff to the water. He was cut on the hands, back, buttocks and crotch area. Evidently he did not jump and free fall into the water as Tammy had done. Instead he slid and fell down the steep cliff slope for 14 meters to the water.

RCMP divers later checked out the bottom for evidence but found nothing. There was about 5 meters of water at the cliff's bottom the evening Tammy drowned.

RCMP investigators from St. John's Criminal Operations now took over the investigation. It was called a sudden death investigation, not a murder, for there was no real evidence of foul play. Sergeant Randy Hogg and Corporal Randy Mercer made another attempt to interview Albert. He declined to provide any statement other than to tell the officers that what he had already said was true. They requested that he undergo a polygraph, or lie detector test. He declined.

An autopsy was performed on Tammy's body at 2:15 p.m. the next day at the Health Sciences Centre in St. John's. A Black Horse beer label was found in her coat pocket.

In their subsequent search of the cabin, the RCMP found a large wine bottle with a small amount of wine remaining, and a case of Black Horse beer with two full and ten empty bottles. Finally, they noticed that one of the bottles had the label removed.

The coroner had requested to be flown to the site of Tammy's death before completing his report. He examined the site, the cliff, and of course, her poor body. He finally concluded that the cause of death was suicide.

Green soon sent to St. John's his final report of the case. He noted that Albert Weller had once again been questioned:

> Personal effects of Albert Weller returned to him at his request. He was spoken to once more about possibly providing a statement concerning any sexual activity he may have had with Tammy King. He was asked again if he would undergo a polygraph examination.

He advised that did not wish to speak to the police about any sexual activity between himself and Tammy King and did not wish to have a polygraph examination.

There does not at this time appear to be any further avenues of investigation to follow up on. There is nothing to suggest that the death of Tammy King was anything other than suicide.

Colin Flynn, the director of Public Prosecutions in Newfoundland, was not satisfied with the case nor the conclusion. He ordered a Judicial Inquiry into the circumstances surrounding Tammy's death. It was to be chaired by Judge LeClair.

It took place on February 21, 22, and March 22, 1989 at the provincial court in Baywood. It was not widely publicized and few people knew about it.

Peter King, Tammy's uncle, was incensed that the social workers had not been called to testify before the Inquiry. In deference to his wishes, Judge LeClair re-convened the Inquiry for an extra day on March 22, when Edith Decker testified.

The bottom line of it all was that everyone involved in Tammy's death could explain away their responsibility, like "Who killed cock robin?" Social Services, RCMP, Janeway, foster homes, school, church, society, everyone was exonerated. We all got away with it.

Now, no one wants to talk about it. A shroud of silence covers the whole unsettling affair. "Everything turns away from the disaster."

Luckily, the Hughes Inquiry convened the next year and took an interest in Tammy's story, also at the prompting of her family. Constable Ron Green, the investigating officer, appeared and testified before the commission.

When he appeared before Justice Hughes, and the Channel 9 camera, Green looked a boyish thirty-six. He was slight in build, and wore large glasses which made his face appear small and somewhat bookish.

He looked like a serious and rather nervous man as he answered the questions of Co-Council Clitus Rowe. Green's thin fingers turned the pages of Profile # 13, a compilation of the files about Tammy, as he dutifully followed the lawyer's direction.

His body sometimes squirmed in his chair as he answered questions about his role in the tragedy. He was one of the most palpably uncomfortable witnesses to appear before the Commission of Inquiry. At times he appeared vague and sometimes appeared not to understand the lawyer's questions.

Green had interviewed Ann Wicks on August 17 when she had described the sexual assaults and named Albert Weller. But Green had not shown up at the Weller home until September 6. He was asked about his twenty-day delay in questioning Albert Weller.

He explained that normal workload and other cases kept him occupied. The Hughes Commission of Inquiry reported:

"These (other cases) included investigations of theft, fire at an abandoned cabin, traffic detail and office work relating to ongoing files. He said there is no real list of priority in relation to files or offenses and he simply did not have the time to interview the suspect."

His superior, Sergeant Don Hilton also appeared before Justice Hughes in relation to this case. Hilton supported his junior officer. He pointed out that the only allegation of abuse in the case had come from Ann Wicks. She was the alleged victim, and the case being investigated, not Tammy or Maggie. Ann was then out of the foster home and in no immediate danger.

In fact Social Services had assured him that the two King girls were safe. He felt that it was the role of the RCMP to investigate the complaint from Ann Wicks but not to become involved in the welfare of the children then in the foster home. That was the role of the Social Services Department.

Sergeant Hilton, therefore did not see the case as urgent. He stated before the Hughes Commission, "The investigation would be done when the time was available to us."

The Commission was then surprised at the subsequent appearance of another RCMP officer who said the exact opposite. Superintendent Emerson Kaiser, was the officer in charge of Criminal Operations Branch, "B" Division. He had the Inquiry buzzing when he appeared shortly after Green and Hilton to say:

> There is no way I can conclude that our response was as timely and appropriate as it should have been. Prudence would caution me that other people in that home are at risk ... and would have driven me to act with much greater haste.... On the facts the only conclusion that I can come to is that we should have reacted with greater dispatch.

Superintendent Kaiser told Justice Hughes that the timeliness and reasonableness of the response by the investigator did not meet the test of then existing RCMP policy. The superintendent felt that Albert Weller should have been apprehended and charged on August 17, 1988.

Constable Green was subsequently promoted to Corporal and placed in charge of another RCMP detachment in Newfoundland. He has since transferred to British Columbia.

Superintendent Kaiser has retired to the Bra d'Or Lakes of Nova Scotia.

Justice Hughes commented on the lack of cooperation between the RCMP and the Social Services Department. The need for effective protocols between the two agencies of public safety are obvious in the case of Tammy King. Hughes concluded:

> This case highlights the necessity for clear guidelines in situations where police and social services responsibilities overlap. Children in foster homes are under the care of the director of child welfare. When a criminal act is alleged ... the police must investigate and social services must be notified. Each has a mandate to fulfil and every effort made to ensure responses are coordinated.

> A social worker should never be placed
> in the position of having to confront alone a
> suspect with an allegation of crime. A police
> officer should be present if only to prevent a
> possible breach of the peace.

Hughes felt that the lack of cooperation between RCMP and Social Services was a factor in this tragedy. Sergeant Hilton's laconic summation, "They got their job to do and we got ours," reflected a great divide between those two agencies.

Differences between the two groups did not stop at their job descriptions. Almost without exception the RCMP officers were male and the Social Services workers were female. This gender identification may have spilled over into the self image and collective image of both groups.

Secondly, there were also the differences in training separating the groups. The university degree program of at least four or five years for Social Services contrasted to the six month quickie of the RCMP. Of course, both groups benefited from on the job training and upgrading courses later in their careers.

Thirdly, most social workers who appeared were articulate and professional. They spoke candidly and directly to the questions.

The RCMP officers, especially in the lower ranks, were less articulate, poised and direct. It should be noted that the two caseworkers for Social Services did not appear before Hughes, while their superiors did. Justice Hughes did not subpoena witnesses; all were volunteers. Every RCMP officer involved appeared before Hughes.

Things did change at the Department of Social Services. As a result of Tammy's death, if an allegation is now made against a foster parent, the present children are immediately removed. It is a sweeping action made necessary by the lack of workers and the case overloads. It can cause problems in some cases but is thought of as preferable to err on the side of caution.

Edith Decker is still a social worker in the St. John's offices. Madonna Hynes is a social worker in Nova Scotia.

Albert Weller was never charged with any crime against Tammy King. On February 5, 1990, he was sentenced to two years for sexual assaults against Ann Wicks, his previous foster daughter. He was also found guilty of sexual assault against Maggie King. He was sentenced to an additional one month in jail, but it was served concurrently with his previous sentence. He is presently living in Deep Harbour.

Alice Weller divorced Albert and re-married. She is living in Deep Harbour with her new husband.

Allan Weller was charged with sexual assault against Maggie King, but the charges were "stayed" because of his advanced years and deafness. He is still living at home in Deep Harbour.

Billy Weller was charged with sexual assault against Dawn Williams. The charges are in limbo, somewhere in the Department of Justice. It seems he was a minor when he "allegedly" abused Dawn Williams. Allan was too old and Billy Weller to young to face the retribution of the courts.

Levi Weller was just the right age for the courts. He was charged and found guilty of sexual assault against Dawn Williams on April 21, 1992. He was sentenced to eighteen months in jail. Levi served four months of his sentence and was then released on day parole on August 28, 1992.

Frank Weller was tried and found guilty of one count of sexual assault against Maggie.

What about the survivors?

When I last spoke with her, Ann Wicks was involved in a civil suit against her two foster homes, the Janeway hospital and the Department of Social Services. She appeared to be in a stable relationship with a sensible young man.

Dawn Williams was pregnant again and living on social assistance. She had recently quit her secretarial course at Trades School. She had an eight year old daughter, Shanna, whom she was raising with her boyfriend, Bill. Her subsequent relationships have been strained and difficult.

Often she cried into the night after Shanna was asleep. She has frequent flashbacks to the sexual abuse and described a nightmarish image that haunted her. She was often depressed, upset and sometimes contemplated suicide.

There's no balance in my life. I can't get my feet on the ground. I can't change it. I can't trust anyone ... I hurt anyone foolish enough to love me. I am an emotional abuser ... I wish I could get the anger out, because I think a lot of my own pain would come out with it.

I tried therapy, but it was too painful. I would spend a week gearing myself up for that hour of therapy. I would cry and come out a wreck. It took me a week to get over it. Maybe some day.

Maggie King was living in a foster home in Deer Lake. A week after Tammy died, Maggie was alone in her room going through Tammy's personal effects packed by Alice Weller and given to the Social Workers. In a small purse she found Tammy's wallet.

Opening the wallet Maggie found pictures of Albert Weller. Her heart stopped.

On the inside pouch of the wallet something, a piece of paper, could barely be seen, tucked carefully away.

Maggie tore the wallet into halves as she frantically tugged to get out the paper. She longed to know what exactly had happened to her sister on the cliff of Rocky Cove Point.

Was she murdered? Was there a suicide pact in which one person reneged? Was she in love with Albert Weller?

There were three sheets of paper torn out of her small diary. Tammy's writing was on each sheet. In this private testament the fifteen year old recorded her love for someone:

"I love this man _____ _____." The letters were omitted but the blanks numbered out the letters in Albert Weller's name. Maggie stared transfixed at the crumpled paper as she read her dead sister's writing. The juvenile testament goes on to describe Tammy's hopes for her love with this unnamed, married man.

Maggie shook with emotion as she read the diary pages. The

remainder of Tammy's diary was never received by Maggie or her family. Nor were the last letters to her family, written the night before Tammy died, nor the other pages of doodling and jotting that she often did.

Maggie kept the "little notes" for a few days and then she turned them over to her social worker in Deer Lake, Don Evans. She understood from Evans that the notes would be sent to Baywood to aid in the prosecution of Albert Weller. That was the last time Maggie saw the notes. Both she and her older sister, Bonny, have to this date been unsuccessful in having those personal effects returned from Social Services.

Did Albert Weller murder Tammy? I do not think so, but there are many questions that I cannot answer about his actions that day: Why did he bring a distraught teenager threatening suicide to the top of a cliff? Why bring her to the only spot in the area where one could jump or fall straight down to the water? Why did he, a trained park warden, not try mouth to mouth resuscitation? Why did Tammy have a cut on her head if she jumped straight down to the water? Why did he refuse to take the polygraph test?

Tammy King is buried in the Anglican Cemetery on Kenmount Road in St. John's, the town of her birth fifteen years before.

I recently walked through the gate and followed the main path down the centre of the cemetery. It was a warm September day with about an hour of sun left in the western sky. I had been years looking for her in the writing of my book.

I had learned much about Tammy Ann King in those years. I had also learned much about the criminal justice system and the social welfare system. I had learned about the human frailties of their officers.

Dag Hammarskjold wrote that the longest journey is the journey inward. I had, as well, learned much about sexual abuse. I had travelled a long way in terms of my own understanding of people like Tammy and Albert. I had learned about my false modesty and how the ogre of secrecy uses it to preserve sexual abuse.

Most of all I had learned about silence and how it is always the most comfortable choice for us all. However, the price of our brief comfort is paid by our children in misery and abuse. This book became my small stand against that overwhelming silence.

I also know the price paid by those who speak out. I met women and men who had been sexually abused as children, often by relatives. Summoning all the courage they possessed they spoke out and named their abusers. In some cases they pursued their nightmares through the courts to a final verdict. Sometimes the abusers went free and at others they were found guilty. Often their communities and families turned against them in defence of their tormentors.

The graveyard path was worn and dry. The treeless place, the fence, the horizon was pleasant with an emphasis on the many horizontal lines.

The only vertical lines in view were the single visitor and the upright headstones. Tammy's headstone suddenly appeared at the very end of the path. Slightly taller than the rest, it has a firm black lettering on subdued grey marble. It stands at the back against an expanse of open ground, so quiet and tall and beautiful, just like Tammy.

INDEX

NOTES

Please use this form to send your comment on my book.
Mail to:

Tom Moore
8 Renews Street
St. John's, NF, Canada
A1E 3R8

Comment: _____

_____

_____

Where did you hear about the book? _____

_____

Why did you read it? _____

_____

Shall I send you a note when my next book is published?

❑ Yes   ❑ No

Please send me immediately an autographed copy of "Angels Crying". I enclose my cheque ❑ money order ❑ for $19.95 incl. tax and postage.

NAME _____

ADDRESS _____

CITY _____ PROV/STATE _____

CODE/ZIP _____